A PEAK DISTRICT ANTHOLOGY

A PEAK DISTRICT ANTHOLOGY

A LITERARY COMPANION TO BRITAIN'S FIRST NATIONAL PARK

Compiled by Roly Smith

FRANCES LINCOLN LIMITED
PUBLISHERS

Frances Lincoln Ltd
4 Torriano Mews
Torriano Avenue,
London NW5 2RZ
www.franceslincoln.com

A Peak District Anthology

First Frances Lincoln edition 2012

A catalogue record for this book is available from the British Library

ISBN 978-0-7112-2887-0

Printed in China

9 8 7 6 5 4 3 2 1

Title page: Hen Cloud, The Roaches (Karen Frenkel)

CONTENTS

INTRODUCTION: FROM WONDERS TO WANDERERS

Unlike the Lake District, the Yorkshire Dales and Snowdonia, the Peak does not seem to have attracted the most famous artists of the late eighteenth century.

It was left to local artists Thomas Smith (d. 1767) and Joseph Wright (1734–97), both of Derby, and Sir Francis Chantrey (1781–1841) of Norton, near Sheffield, to be the first to capture the scenic wonders of the Peak. Having said that, the French artist Philip James de Loutherbourg (1740–1812), a designer at the Drury Lane Theatre, apparantly did produce a rather melodramatic series of backcloths in the 1770s to a pantomine entitled *The Wonders of Derbyshire*.

Joseph Wright's famous study of *Arkwright's Cotton Mills at Cromford by Moonlight* (1783) is one of the first depictions of the Industrial Revolution, and his *Earthstopper on the Banks of the Derwent* (1773) shows the first signs of his use of artificial light to illuminate his pictures.

A young J.M.W. Turner also conducted several tours of the Peak in the early nineteenth century, producing a series of recently discovered sketches of places such as High Tor at Matlock Bath, Castleton, Chatsworth and Haddon. Unfortunately his greatest work in the Peak, an oil painting of an unknown subject simply entitled *Scene in Derbyshire*, which he exhibited at the Royal Academy in 1827, is now lost.

Writers, however, seem to have had no such dread of the 'sublime' landscapes of the Peak. The first written description of countryside that can be positively identified as the Peak was in one of the earliest poems in the English language. The alliterative Arthurian poem *Sir Gawain and the Green Knight* is thought to have been written around

Lud's Church

the year 1400 by an unknown poet, who, judging from his diction, was from somewhere in the north Midlands. According to his latest translator, Simon Armitage, the poet's description of the Green Chapel, scene of the fateful denouement of the piece, seems to match pretty closely with that of the natural fissure of Lud's Church, north of The Roaches in the Staffordshire Moorlands.

Perhaps the 1959 translation by Brian Stone best captures the character of the landscape around Back Forest and The Roaches.

> By bluffs where boughs were bare they passed,
> Climbed by cliffs where the cold clung:
> Under the high clouds, ugly mists
> Merged damply with the moors and melted on the mountains;
> Each hill had a hat, a huge mantle of mist,
> Brooks burst forth above them, boiling over their banks
> And showering down sharply in shimmering cascades.
> Wonderfully wild was their way through the woods;
> Till soon the sun in the sway of that season
> Brought day.

The first description of the 'Seven Wonders of the Peak', which echoed the fabled Seven Wonders of the Ancient World, seems to have be made by the sixteenth-century antiquarian William Camden in his *Britannia,* a history of Britain from pre-Roman times, which was published in 1586.

Camden's description and listing of the wonders was followed by Michael Drayton, the Warwickshire-born poet, in his *Poly-Olbion* (1622), and later by Thomas Hobbes, tutor to the Cavendish children at Chatsworth in 1636, and finally by Charles Cotton, the spendthrift squire of Beresford Hall in Dovedale, in 1682.

Cotton was, of course, the joint author with Izaak Walton of the greatest classic of angling literature, *The Compleat Angler*, based on their piscatorial exploits on the Rivers Dove, Manifold and Lathkill, first published in 1653 and never out of print since. In fact, *The Compleat Angler* is said to be the most republished book in the English language, after the Bible and the Book of Common Prayer.

The publication of lists of wonders seems to have sparked the interests of the first tourists to the Peak District, most notably those intrepid early travellers and topographical writers Celia Fiennes and Daniel Defoe in the early eighteenth century. They followed the itinerary first set by Camden and Drayton in visiting and describing, in Defoe's case with varying degrees of contempt, the Wonders of the Peak.

The coming of the railways – the ambitious Cromford and High Peak Railway opened as early as 1831, only five years after George Stephenson's Stockton to Darlington line – created the next great impetus for writers and tourists. And when the Midland Line reached Rowsley in 1849, the floodgates opened for a rush of visitors from the south and London.

Lord Byron and John Ruskin both extolled the beauties of the Peak, Byron expressing his wonder at the Derbyshire landscape in a much-quoted letter to his friend, the Irish poet Tom Moore, who later came to live at Mayfield, at the entrance to Dovedale. 'Was you ever in Dovedale?'

he enquired. 'I assure you there are things in Derbyshire as noble as in Greece or Switzerland.'

Victorian novelists Charlotte Brontë, George Eliot and Mrs Humphrey Ward used closely observed Peakland settings for some of their most vivid narratives. Topographical writers such as Edward Bradbury (actually an employee of the Midland Railway, who also wrote under the pen name of 'Strephon'), Louis Jennings, Thomas Tudor and James Croston enthusiastically described the delights of the Derbyshire scenery to the ever-increasing stream of Victorian visitors.

The Peak was blessed with a number of talented local writers, such as the children's author Alison Uttley, Crichton Porteous and R. Murray Gilchrist, during that flowering of guidebook and topographical writing in the twentieth century.

It was at this time that the pressure was growing for greater public access to the Peak's highest ground, such as the northern moors of Kinder Scout and Bleaklow and the Eastern Edges. Much of this land was forbidden to the walker since it had been acquired by local landowners after the Enclosure Acts of the eighteenth and nineteenth centuries, mainly to pursue the sport of grouse shooting. 'Trespassers will be Prosecuted' signs – known to ramblers as 'wooden liars' – appeared at most access points, and grim-faced, stick-wielding gamekeepers brutally enforced their masters' will.

This period also saw the flowering of the Peak's outdoor literature, which still rates as among the finest in the country, and many books were produced covertly encouraging what was known as 'the gentle art of trespass'. They included works by G.H.B. Ward, the 'King' of the Sheffield Clarion Ramblers (through fifty years of his famous Clarion handbooks for one of the first working class walking clubs in the country); Derby's pioneering rock climber, Ernest Baker; John Derry, editor of the *Sheffield & Rotherham Independent*; and Patrick Monkhouse, deputy editor of the *Manchester Guardian*. Monkhouse's *On Foot in the Peak* (1932) remains

Fly-fishing on Walton and Cotton's River Dove

one of the finest walking books to the area, even giving ramblers warnings as to where to expect the presence of gamekeepers at busy weekends.

Later writers who have continued this tradition of fine outdoor writing include the Manchester-born, multi-Boardman Tasker Award winner Jim Perrin; *Manchester Evening News* editor and broadcaster Brian Redhead; longstanding *Guardian* Country Diarist Roger Redfern; and Eric Byne and Geoffrey Sutton, whose *High Peak* (1966) first told the epic story of walking and climbing in the Peak.

This anthology is an attempt to bring together some of the finest writing about the Peak District through the ages, illustrated by Karen Frenkel's evocative modern photographs and period engravings and vignettes. It is the compiler's fond hope that it will revive many long-forgotten descriptions of what many people believe is the finest, most varied and best-loved landscape in the whole of Britain.

I.
THE SEVEN WONDERS OF THE PEAK

The first listing of the 'Wonders of the Peak' appears to have be made by William Camden, the sixteenth-century antiquarian, historian and sometime Clarenceux King of Arms, in his Britannia *(1586). Writing, as was the custom at the time, in Latin, he described:*

WILLAM CAMDEN *Britannia* (1586)

Miro alto Pecco tria sunt, barathrum, specus, antrum;
Commoda tot, plumbum, gramen, ovile pecus,
Tota speciosa, simul sunt, Castrum, Balnea, Chatsworth;
Plura sed occurrunt qua septiosa minus.

This loosely translates as:

Nine things that please us at the Peak we see;
A Cave, a Den, a Hole, the Wonder be;
Lead, Sheep and Pasture, are the useful Three.
Chatsworth, the Castle and the Bath delight,
Much more you see; all little worth the Sight.

Obviously heavily influenced by Camden's list, Michael Drayton, a Warwickshire-born poet, also included Mam Tor, the Royal Forest

of the Peak and the Ebbing and Flowing Well in his Poly-Olbion *(1622). His work was illustrated by a highly allegorical map, which owes much more to the imagination than any sense of geographical accuracy and is populated by various nymphs and muses, with the Peak itself represented by a stooping hag.*

MICHAEL DRAYTON *Poly-Olbion* (1622)

A withered bedlam long, with bleared, waterish eyes;
With many a bleak storm dimmed, which often to the skies;
She cast, and oft to th' earth bowed down her aged head;
Her meagre, wrinkled face being sullied still with lead.

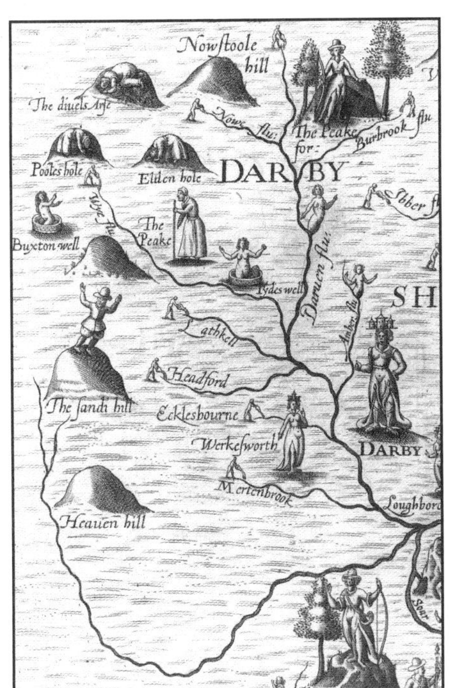

Camden listed the wonders as: The Devil's Arse (Peak Cavern, Castleton); Poole's Hole (Poole's Cavern, Buxton); Eldon Hole (near Peak Forest); Tydeswell (the Ebbing and Flowing Well at Tideswell – or possibly Barmoor Clough); Sandi Hill (Mam Tor, above Castleton), and the Peake Forest.

Michael Drayton's allegorical map of Derbyshire, showing the Seven Wonders

The first real guidebook aimed at tourists to the Peak was written in long-winded Latin hexameters by Thomas Hobbes, the famous philosopher and tutor to the Cavendish children at Chatsworth. His De Mirabilibus Pecci: Concerning the Wonders of the Peak in Darby-shire *was first published in 1636, and in it he listed seven 'wonders' which he had visited during a two-day ride. He described:*

THOMAS HOBBES *De Mirabilibus Pecci* (1636)

Alti censentur septem miracula Pecci,
Aedes, mons, Barathum, binus Fons, antraque bina

Freely translated, this means:

Of the High Peak are seven wonders writ,
Two fonts, two caves, one palace, mount and pit.

The wonders were, in their original order, a house (Chatsworth); a mountain (Mam Tor); a chasm (Eldon Hole); two fountains (St Ann's Well in Buxton and the Ebbing and Flowing Well at Barmoor Clough or Tideswell); and two caves (Poole's Cavern and Peak Cavern).

These wonders, deliberately echoing the Seven Ancient Wonders of the World, were later rehashed in English for the fast-expanding tourist market in 1682, three years after Hobbes's death, by Charles Cotton, the impecunious squire of Beresford Hall in Dovedale and co-author with Izaak Walton of the anglers' bible, The Compleat Angler.

Cotton's essay on The Wonders of the Peake *is dedicated to Elizabeth, Countess Devonshire, and is of full of seventeenth century effulgence. This is an edited version of the poem.*

Eldon Hole

CHARLES COTTON *The Wonders of the Peake* (1682)

Durst I Expostulate with *Providence,*
I then should ask, wherein the Innocence
Of my poor undesigning Infancy,
Could *Heaven* offend to such a black degree,
As for th' offence to damn me to a Place
Where *Nature* only suffers in Disgrace.
A *Country* so Deform'd, the *Traveller*
Would swear those parts *Nature's Pudenda* were:
Like *Warts* and *Wens*, Hills on the *one side* swell,
To all but *Natives* Inaccessible;
Th' other a blue scrofulous Scum defiles,
Flowing from th' Earths impostumated Boyles;
That seems the steps (Mountains on Mountains thrown)
By which the *GIANTS* storm'd the *Thunderers* Throne,
This from that *prospect* seems the *sulph'rous Flood,*
Where sinful *Sodom* and *Gomorrah* stood.

A *Country* that abounds with *Rarities,*
They call them *Wonders* there, and be they so;
But the whole Country sure's a *Wonder* too,
And *Mother* of the rest, which Seven are,
And one of them do singularly Rare,
As does indeed amount to Miracle,
And all the Kingdom boasts so far excel.
It ought not, I confess, to be Profan'd
By my poor *Muse*; nor should an Artless hand
Presume to take a *Crayon* up, to trace
But the faint *Land-scape* of so brave a place.

Yet noble *Chatsworth*, for I speak of thee,
Pardon the Love will prompt the Injury
My Pen must do thee, when, before I end,
I six Dishonour, where I would Commend.

POOLE'S CAVERN

The first of these I meet with in my way,
Is a vast *Cave*, which old People say
One *Poole* an *Out-law* made his Residence;
But why he did so, or for what Offence,
The *Beagles* of the *Law* should press so near,
As, spight of Horrors self, to earth him there,
Is in our times a *Riddle*; and in this
Tradition most unkindly silent is;
But whatsoe're his Crime, than such a Cave
A worse Imprisonment he could not have.

At a high *Mountain's* foot, whose lofty Crest
O're-looks the Marshy Prospect of the *West*;
Under its Base there is an *Overture*
Which Summer Weeds do render so obscure,
The careless *Traveller* may pass, and n'er
Discover, or suspect an entry there:
But such a one there is, as we might well
Think it the *Crypto-porticus* of *Hell*.

ST ANN'S WELL

Six hundred Paces hence, and *Northward* still,
As by the rest of greater bulk, and fame,
Environ'd round, scarcely deserves that Name.

A Crystal *Fountain* springs in healing Streams,
Hot (though closeshaded from the Suns warm Beams,
By a malicious Roof, that covers it,
So close, as not his prying Eye t'admit
That else where Priviledg'd, here to behold
His beamy Face, and Locks of burning Gold.
In the most flatt'ring Mirror, that below
His Travel round the spacious Globe can show)
So fair a *Nymph*, and so supremely bright,
The teeming *Earth* did never bring to light;
Not does the rush into the world with noise
Like *Neptune's* ruder Sex of roaring *Boys*;
But boils and simmers up, as if the heat
That warms her waves that motion did beget.
But where's the Wonder? For it is well known
Warm and clear Fountains in the *Peake* abound,
Each *Yeoman* almost has them in his ground.
Take then the Wonder of this famous place:
This tepid Fountain a *Twin-Sister* has,
Of the same Beauty and Complexion,
That, bubbling Six Foot off, joyns both in one:
But yet so Cold withal, that who will stride
When Bathing, cross the *Bath* but half so wide,
Shall in one Body, which is strange, endure
At once an *Ague* and a *Calenture.*
Strange that Two *Sisters* springing up at once,
Should differ thus is Constitutions;
And would be stranger, could they be the fame.
That Love should have one half of the Heart enflame,
Whilst th' other, senseless of a Lovers pain,

Freezes it felt, and him, in cold Distain;
Or that a *Naiade*, having careless play'd
With some *male wanton Stream*, and fruitful Maid
Should have her silver Breasts at once to flow,
One with *Warn Milk*, th' other with *melted Snow.*

TIDESWELL

North-East from hence three *Peakish* Miles at least,
(Which once measured will dread all the rest)
At th' instep of just such another Hill,
There creeps a Spring that makes a little Rill,
Which at first sight to curious Visitors,
So small, and so contemptible appears,
They'd think themselves *abus'd*, did they not stay
To see wherein the Wonder of it lay.
This Fountain is so very, very small,
Th' Observer hardly can perceive it crawl
Through the sedg, which scarcely in their beds
Confess a Currant by their waving heads.
I'th' Chinks through which it issues to the day,
It *stagnant* seems, and makes so little way,
That Thistle-down without a breeze of Air,
May lie at *Hull*, and be becalmed there;
Which makes the wary Owner of the ground
For his Herds use the tardy Waves impound,
In a low *Cistern* of so small content
As stops so little of the *Element*
For so important use, that when the *Cup*
Is fullest crown'd, a *Cow* may drink it up.
Yet this so still, so very little Well,

Which thus beheld seems so Contemptible,
No less of real *Wonder* does comprize,
Than any of the other *Rarities:*
For now and then, a hollow murmuring Sound,
Being first heard remotely underground,
The Spring immediately swells, and straight
Boils up through several Pores to such a height,
As, overflowing soon the narrow *Shoar*,
Below does in a little *Torrent* Roar.
Thorough the secret *Conduits* of her Springs,
With such a Harmony of various Notes,
As *Grotto's* yeild, through narrow Brazen throats
When, by weight of higher Streams, the lower
Are upwards forc'd in an inverted shower,
But the sweet *Musick's* short, three minutes space
To highest *Mark* this *Occanet* does raise,
And half that Time retires the ebbing Waves,
To the dark windings of their frigid *Caves.*

ELDON HOLE

Hence two miles *East*, does a fourth *Wonder* lye,
Worthy the greatest Curiosity,
Call'd *Elden-Hole*; but such a dreadful Place,
As will procure a Tender *Muse* her grace,
In the Description if she chance to fail,
When my *Hand* Trembles, & my *Cheeks* turn pale.
Betwixt a verdant *Mountains* falling Flanks,
And within Bounds of easie swelling Banks,
That hem the *Wonder* in on either side,
A Formidable *Scissure* gapes so wide,

Steep, Black, and full of Horror, that who dare
Looks down into the *Chasme*, and keeps his Hair
From lifting off his Hat, either has none,
Or for more Modish Curls cashiers his own.
It were injurious, I must confess,
By mine to measure braver Courages:
But when I peep into't, I must declare,
My *Heart* still beats, and *Eyes* with horror flare.
And he, that standing on the Brink of *Hell*,
Can carry it so unconcern'd, and well,
As to betray no Fear, is, certainly,
A better *Christian*; or a worse than *I*.

This yawning Mouth is thirty paces long,
Scarce half so wide, within lin'd through with strong
Continuous Walls of solid perpend Stone:
A Gulf wide, steep, black, and a dreadful one:
Which few that comes to see it dare come near,
And the more daring still approach with fear,
Having with terror, held beheld a Space,
The gastly Aspect of this dangerous Place;
Critcial *Passengers* usually found,
How deep the threatening *Gulph* goes *under-ground*
By tumbling down stones sought throughout the Field,
As great as the officious *Boores* can wield,
Of which such *Millions* of *Tuns* are thrown,
That in a *Country*, almost all of Stone,
About the *place* they something scarce are grown
But being brought, down they'r condemn'd to go
When *Silence* being made, and Ears laid low,

The first's turn'd off, which, as it parts the Air,
A kind of *Sighing* makes, as if it were
Capable of that useless Passion, *Fear*,
Till the first hit strikes the astonisht Ear,
Like *Thunder* under-ground; thense it invades,
With louder Thunders, those *Tararean* shades,
Which groan forth *horror*, at each *ponderous stroke,*
Th' unnatural *Issue* gives the *Parent* Rock;
Whilst, as it strikes, the sound by turns we note,
When nearer *flat, sharper* when more remote,
As the hard walls, on which it strikes, are found
Fit to reverberate the bellowing sound:
When, after falling long, it seems to hiss,
Like the Old *Serpent* in a Dark *Abyss:*
Till *Eccho*, tir'd with posting, does refuse
To carry to th' inquisitive *Perdu's,*
That couchant lye above, the trembling news.
And there ends our Intelligence; how far
It travels further, no one can declare;
Though if it rested here, the place might well
Sure be accepted for a *Miracle.*

Your *Guide* to all these Wonders, never fails
To entertain you with ridic'lous Tales
Of this strange place, one of the *Goose* thrown in,
Which out of *Peaks-Arse* [Peak Cavern], two miles off, was seen
Shell-naked sally, rifled of her Plume;
By which a man may lawfully presume,
The Owner was a Woman grave, and wife,
Could know her *Goose* again in that disguise.

MAM TOR

Enough of *Hell!* From hence you forward ride;
Still mounting up the *Mountains* groaning side,
Till having gain'd the utmost height, your Eye
North-ward a mile a higher does descry,
And steeper much, tho' from that prospect green,
With a Black, moorish Valley stretcht between.
Unlike in stature, and in substance, this
To the *South-east* is a great Precipice
Not of firm Rock, like the rest here that shroud
Their lowring *Summits* in a dewy Cloud:
But of a shaly Earth, that from the Crown
With a continual motion mouldring down,
Spawns a less *Hill* of looser mould below,
Which will in time tall as the Mother grow,
And must perpetuate the *Wonder* so.
Which *Wonder* is, that tho this Hill ne'r cease
To waste it self, it suffers no Decrease:
But t'would a greater be, if those that pass
Should miss the *Atomes* of so vast a *Mass*:
Tho *Neighbours* if they nearer would enquire,
Must needs perceive the pilling *Cliff* retire:
And the most cursory beholder may
Visibly see a manifest decay,
By Jutting Stones, that by the Earth left bare,
Hang on the tip suspended in the Air.
This haughty Mountain by indulgent *Fame*
Perfer'd t'a *Wonder, Mam-Tor* has to Name,
For in that Country *Jargon's* uncouth Sense
Expressing any Craggy Eminence,

From *Tower*; but then why *Mam*, I can't surmise,
Unless because *Mother* to that does rise
Out of her Ruins; better then to speak,
It might be call'd the *Phoenix* of the *Peake*;
For when this *Mountain* by long Waiting's gone;
Her Ashes will, and not till then be one.

PEAK CAVERN

Hence an uneven mile below, in sight
Of this strange *Cliff*, and almost opposite,
Lies *Castleton* a Place of Noted Fame,
Which from the *Castle* there derives its Name.
Entring the *Village* presently ye're met
With a clear, swift and murm'ring *Rivulet*,
Towards whole *Source* if up the stream you look,
On your right hand close by, your Eye is strook

Peak Cavern

With a stupendous Rock, raising so high
His craggy *Temples* tow'rds the Azure Sky,
That if we this should with the rest compare,
They *Hillocks, Mole-hills, Warts* and *Pibbles* are.
This, as if *King* of all the *Mountains* round,
Is on the top with an Old *Tower* Crown'd,
An *Antick* thing, fit to male People stare:
But of no use, either in Peace, or War.
Under this *Castle* yawns a dreadful *Cave*
Whose sight may well astonish the most brave,
And make him pause, ere further he proceed
T'explore what in those gloomy Vaults lie hid.

Now to the *Cave* we come, wherein is found
A new strange thing, a *Village under ground*;
Houses and *Barns* for *Men*, and *Beasts behoof*,
With distinct *Walls*, under *one solid Roof*.
Stacks both of *Hay* and *Turf*, which yields a scent,
Can only fume from *Satan's* Fundament;
For this *black Cave* lives in the voice of *Fame*,
To the same sense by yet a coarser *Name*.

The *Subterranean People* ready stand,
A Candle each, most two in either hand,
To guide, who are to penetrate inclin'd,
The *Intestinum Rectum* of the *Fiend*.
Thus, by a blinking and promiseuous Light,
We now begin to travel into *Night*,
Hoping indeed to see the *Sun* agen;
Tho none of us can tell, or how, or when.

CHATSWORTH

Southward from hence ten miles, where *Derwent* laves
His broken Shores with never clearing Waves,
There stands a stately, and stupendous *Pile*
Like the proud *Regent* of the *Brittish* Isle,
Shedding her Beams over the Barren Vale,
Which else bleak *Winds*, and nipping *Frosts* assail
With such perpetual *War*, there would appear
Nothing but *Winter* ten months of the year.

This *Palace*, with wild prospects girded round,
Stands in the middle of a falling ground,
At a black *Mountains* foot, whose craggy Brow
Secures from *Eastern Tempests* all below,
Under whose shelter *Trees* and *Flowers* grow,
With early *Blossoms*, maugre native Snow;
Which else-where round a *Tyranny* maintains,
And binds crampt *Nature* long in *Crystal-Chains*.
The *Fabrick's* noble Front faces the *West*,
Turning her fair broad shoulders to the *East*,
On the *South-side* the stately *Gardens* lye,
Where the scorn'd *Peak* rivals proud *Italy*.
And on the *North* sev'ral inferior *Plots*
For servile use scatter'd do lye in spots.

To view from hence the glittering *Pile* above
(Which must at once Wonder create and Love)
Environ'd round with natures Shames, and Ills,
Black Heaths, wild Rock, bleak Craggs and naked Hills,
And the whole *Prospect* so inform, and rude

Who is it, but must presently conclude?
That this is *Paradice*, which seated stands
In midst of *Desarts*, and of barren *Sands*.
So bright a *Diamond* would look is set
In a vile *socket* of ignoble *Jet*,
And such a face the new born *Nature* took,
When out of *Chaos*, by the *Fiat* strook.
Doubtless, if any where, there never yet
So brave a *Structure* on such ground was set,
Which sure the *Foundress* built, to reconcile
This to the other members of the *Isle*,
And would remain therein, first her own *Grandeur* show,
And then what *Art* could, spite of *Nature*, do.

The tour of the Seven Wonders of the Peak soon became an accepted and fashionable itinerary for early visitors, including Edward Browne, later to be physician to Charles II, who travelled all the way from Norwich to see them in 1622. He was impressed by 'this strange, mountainous, misty, moorish, rocky wild country' with its 'craggy ascents, the rocky unevenness of the roade, the high peaks and the almost perpendicular descents'.

Celia Fiennes, the redoubtable daughter of a Roundhead colonel and the first in a long line of this adventurous Oxfordshire family, rode through the Peak alone and by side-saddle with the object of visiting the Wonders in 1698. She recorded her impressions in Through England on a Side Saddle in the Time of William and Mary. *Fiennes, like Browne, was most impressed by the steep and dangerous terrain she encountered. As she famously wrote:*

CELIA FIENNES *Through England on a Side Saddle in the Time of William and Mary* (1698)

All Derbyshire is full of steep hills, and nothing but the peakes of hills as thick one by another is seen in most of the County which are very steepe which makes travelling tedious, and the miles long, you see neither hedge nor tree but only low drye stone walls round some ground, else its only hills and dales as thick as you can imagine . . .

Fiennes visited the wonders of Chatsworth, St Ann's Well, Poole's Cavern, Eldon Hole, Mam Tor, Peak Cavern and the Ebbing and Flowing Well, But her view of the wonder of Eldon Hole is a little more jaundiced than that of Hobbes and Cotton.

The 4th Wonder is that of Elden Hole; it's on the side of a hill about 30 yards if not better in length at the brim, and half so broad, and just in sight is full of craggy stones like a rock for about 2 or 3 yards down, which contracts the Mouth of the Hole to about 4 yards long and 2 broad or thereabouts, which Hole is suppos'd to run down directly a vast length and has been try'd with a line and plummet severall fathom and the bottom not sounded; tho' some are of the opinion its because the hole runns aslant so the plummet and line could not pass, and what we observ'd gives some strength to this notion, for cast a stone down you hear it strike a long tyme at the sides of the hole and if you go down below 100 yards or more and lay your head to the ground you shall hear the stone ring much longer than those that stand at the Holes mouth, which must discover the ground to be hollow at least much farther in compass than the mouth of the Hole; it's a very hazardous place, for if man or beast be too near the edge of the bank and trip they fall in without retrieve; the beasts graze in the grounds and hills but it must be some great force that drives them near the Hole; there is a sort of instinct in Nature self preservation and a great sence of danger in beasts; its reported that severall attempts have been made to fence the whole round with a stone wall as the manner of the fences are all over that Country but that it has all been in vaine, what they built up in the day would be pull'd down in the night…

Fiennes' description of Mam Tor, the so-called 'Shivering Mountain', is still one of the most original, and takes some beating:

The fifth Wonder is Mamtour [Mam Tor] which is a high hill that looks exactly round but on the side next [to] Castleton, which is a little town in the high peake, on that side its all broken that it looks just in resemblance as a great Hay-Ricke that's cut down one halfe, on one side that describes it most naturall, this is all sand, and on that broken side the sand keeps trickling down allwayes especially when there is the least wind, of which I believe this Country scarce ever is without, many places of the hill looks hollow and loose which makes it very dangerous to ascend and none does attempt it, the sand being loose slips the foote back againe.

Fiennes is less squeamish than her successor Daniel Defoe (see below) in describing Peak Cavern, then commonly (and again more recently) known as the Devil's Arse.

. . . this is what they call the Devills Arse a Peake, the hill on one end jutting out in two parts and joyns in one at the top, this part or cleft between you enter a great Cave which is very large, and severall poor little houses in it built of stone and thatch'd like little Styes, one seemed a little bigger in which a Gentleman liv'd and his wife that was worth above £100 a year which he left to his brother chooseing rather like a hermit to live in this sorry cell; one Mr. Midleton who was with us said he had dined with them there on carrots and herbs, and that he was dead and his wife a year or two since; now none but very poor people live there which makes some small advantage by begging and by lighting the strangers into the Cave . . .

She was also a little sceptical of Tideswell's Ebbing and Flowing Well, said to be governed by the rising and falling of the tides.

The Seventh Wonder is a Flowing and Ebbing Well which ceases its miraculous motion but on great raines which raises the springs, and then the man which was with us told me he had seen it severall tymes in the winter when the springs were high to Ebb and Flow severall tymes an hour, which appear'd by the rise and fall of the water from the edge of the well – and the man seem'd to be a good sober man Mr Middleton it was – so that its likely when the springs are high the water from the sea may have a quicker flux and reflux thro' the Channells of the Earth but this is a good distance from the sea of ebbing and flowing rivers.

Celia Fiennes was followed twenty years later by Daniel Defoe, the journalist and political commentator, who is probably best known for his story of the castaway, Robinson Crusoe. *His* Tour thro'the Whole Island of Great Britain, *first published in instalments between 1724 and 1726, systematically debunked Hobbes' and Cotton's 'Wonders' in pretty scathing terms, concluding that only Eldon Hole and Chatsworth – 'one a wonder of nature, the other of art' – were worthy of the name.*

It is fair to say that Defoe, who tended to look at the world only in terms of its economic potential, was not exactly enamoured of the Peak District in any case. He described the inhabitants, and in particular the lead miners, as 'a rude boorish kind of people' and reckoned that their ancient Barmoot Court, which attempted to govern the activities of these people of 'a strange, turblent, quarrelsome temper', was 'the greatest of all the wonders of the Peak'.

Defoe described the landscape as 'a waste and houling wilderness, over which when strangers travel, they are obliged to take guides, or it would be next to impossible not to lose their way'. The High Peak, he wrote, was perhaps . . .

DANIEL DEFOE *Tour Thro' the Whole Island of Great Britain* (1726)

. . . the most desolate, wild and abandoned country in all England; the mountains of the Peak, of which I have been speaking, seem to be but the beginning of wonders to this part of the country, and but the beginning of mountains, or, if you will, as the lower rounds of a ladder. The tops of these hills seem to be as much above the clouds, as the clouds are above the ordinary range of hills.

Defoe pours scorn on the Wonders as soon as he enters the Peak District, as if he can't wait to sharpen the nib of his satirical pen and get to work on the systematic demolition of the ideas of Hobbes and Cotton.

And now I am come to this wonderful place, the Peak, where you will expect I should do as some others have, (I think, foolishly) done before me, viz. tell you strange long stories of wonders as (I must say) they are most weakly call'd; and that you may not think me arrogant in censuring so many wise men, who have wrote of these wonders, as if they were all fools . . .

After correctly crediting Camden with the first listing of the Wonders, Defoe then starts to discredit both Hobbes and Cotton for perpetuating the myths:

Now to have so great a man as Mr. Hobbes, and after him Mr. Cotton, celebrate the trifles here, the first in a fine Latin poem, the last in English verse, as if they were the most exalted wonders of the world: I cannot but, after wondering at their making wonders of them, desire you, my friend, to travel with me through this houling wilderness in your imagination, and you shall soon find all that is wonderful about it.

He visited the village (as it was then) of Buxton, dismissing its wonders of St Ann's Well and Poole's Cavern, first.

. . . Buxton bath (St Ann's Well), which they call one of the wonders of the Peak; but it is so far from being a wonder, that to us, who had been at Bath in Somersetshire, and at Aix la Chapelle in Germany, it was nothing at all; nor it is any thing but what is frequent in such mountainous countries as this is, in many parts of the world.

That which was more wonderful to me than all of it, was, that so light is made of them as to use; that the people rather wonder at them than take benefit of them; and that, as there are several hot springs in the village of Buxton, as well as at Matlock . . . and at several other places, they are not built into noble and convenient bathing places; and, instead of a house or two, a city built there for the entertainment of company; which, if it were done, and countenance given to it, as it is to the baths at Bath, I doubt not it would be as well frequented, and to good purpose.

Buxton had to wait another sixty years for the 5th Duke of Devonshire, using the huge profits made from his mineral rights in the Peak, especially the copper mines of Ecton Hill in the Manifold Valley, to develop the town as a fashionable spa in the late eighteenth century.

But though I shall not treat this warm spring as a wonder, for such it is not; I must nevertheless give it praise due to the medicinal virtues of its waters; for it is not to be deny'd, but that wonderful cures have been wrought by them, especially in rheumatick, scorbutick and scrofolous distempers, aches of the joints, nervous pains, and also in scurfy and leprous maladies.

South west from hence, about a quarter of a mile, or not so much, on the side, or rather at the foot of a very high ridge of mountains, is a great cave or hole in the earth, called Poole's Hole, another of the wonderless wonders of the Peak. The wit that has been spent upon this vault or cave in the earth, had been well enough to raise the expectations of strangers, and bring fools a great way to creep into it; but is ill bestowed upon all those that come to the place with a just curiosity, founded upon antient report; when these go in to see it, they generally go away, acknowledging that they have seen nothing suitable to their great expectation, or to the fame of the place.

It is a great cave, or natural vault, antient doubtless as the mountain itself, and occasioned by the fortuitous position of the rocks at the creation of all things, or perhaps at the great rupture of the earth's crust or shell, according to Mr Burnet's theory; and to me it seems a confirmation of that hypothesis of the breaking in of the surface.

It may be deepen'd and enlarged by streams and eruptions of subterranean waters, of which here are several, as there generally are in all such cavities; as at Castleton in this country, at Wooky Hole in Somersetshire . . . and at several other like caves which are now to be seen among the mountains in Switzerland, in Norway, in Hungary, and other places.

The story of one Pole or Poole, a famous giant or robber, (they might as well have called him a man eater) who harboured in this vault, and whose kitchen and lodging, or bed chamber, they show you on your right-hand, after you have crept about ten yards upon all-four; I say, this I leave to those who such stories are better suited to, than I expect of my readers.

However, this helps among people there, to make out the *wonder*; and indeed such things are wanting where really wonder is wanting, else there would be no wonder at all in it; as indeed there is not.

We saw indeed a variety of objects here; some that came purely for the pleasure of bathing, taking the air, and to see the country, which has many things rare and valuable to be seen, tho' nothing, as I met with, can be called a wonder . . .

Passing on to Castleton he came to two more 'wonderless' wonders: the so-called 'Shivering Mountain' of Mam Tor which overlooks the village, and Peak Cavern, now claimed to be the largest cave entrance in Britain.

The first of these is Mam Tor, or, as the word in the mountain jargon signifies, the Mother Rock, upon a suggestion that the soft crumbling earth, which falls from the summit of the one, breeds or begets several young mountains below. The sum of the wonder is this, that there is a very high hill, nay, I will add (that I may make the most of the story, and that it may appear as much like a wonder as I can) an exceeding high hill. But this in a country which is all over hills, cannot be much of a wonder, because there are several higher hills in the Peak than that, only just not there.

. . . Nothing is more certain than this, that the more water comes down from it, the less remains in it; and so it certainly is of Mam Tor, in spite of all the poetry of Mr. Cotton or Mr. Hobbes, and in spight (sic) of all the women's tales in the Peak.

This hill lies on the north side of the road from Buxton to Castleton, where we come to the so famed wonder call'd, saving our good manners, *The Devil's A—e in the Peak*; Now notwithstanding the grossness of the name given it, and that there is nothing of similitude or coherence either in form or figure, or any other thing between the thing signified and the thing signifying; yet we must search narrowly for any thing in it to make a wonder, or even any thing so strange, or odd, or vulgar, as the name would seem to import.

The short of this story is; that on the steep side of a mountain there is a large opening very high, broad at the bottom, and narrow, but rounding, on the top, almost the form of the old Gothick gates or arches, which come up, not to a half circle or half oval at the top, but to a point; though this being all wild and irregular, cannot be said to be an arch, but a meer chasme, entring horizontally; the opening being upwards of thirty foot perpendicular, and twice as much broad at the bottom at least.

The arch continues thus wide but a little way, yet far enough to have several small cottages built on either side of it within the entrance; so that 'tis like a little town in a vault: In the middle (as it were a street) is a running stream of water; the poetical descriptions of it will have this called a river, tho' they have not yet bestow'd a name on it, nor indeed is it worthy of a name.

In Victorian times, it indeed became known as the River Styx, one of the Greek legendary rivers of Hades, across which Charon ferried the spirits of the dead.

If there were no such vaults and arches any where but in the Peak, or indeed if they were not frequent in such mountainous countries, as well here, as in other nations, we might call this a wonder. But as we know they are to be found in many places in England, and that we read of them in the description of other countries, and even in the Scripture, we cannot think there is any room to call it a wonder.

The next wonder, which makes up number five, is called Tideswell, or a spring of water which ebbs and flows, as they will have it, as the

Chatsworth

sea does. A poor thing indeed to make a wonder of; and therefore most of the writers pass over it with little notice; only that they are at a loss to make the number up to seven without it.

So much for the ficticious wonders, or indeed simple wonders. The two real wonders which remain, are first, Elden Hole, and secondly, the Duke of Devonshire's fine house at Chatsworth; one a wonder of nature, the other of art. I begin with the last.

Chatsworth is indeed a most glorious and magnificent house, and, as it has had two or three founders, may well be said to be completely designed and finished.

It is indeed a palace for a prince, a most magnificent building, and, in spite of all the difficulties or disadvantages of situation, is a perfect beauty; nay the very obstructions and, as I called them, disadvantages of its situation, serve to set off its beauty, and are, by the most exquisite decoration of the place, made to add to the lustre of the whole.

Nothing can be more surprising of its kind, than for a stranger coming from the north, suppose from Sheffield in Yorkshire, for that is the first town of note, and wandering or labouring to pass this difficult desert country, and seeing no end to it, and almost discouraged and beaten out with the fatigue of it (just such was our case) on a sudden the guide brings him to this precipice, where he looks down from a frightful height, and a comfortless, barren, and, as he thought, endless moor, into the most delightful valley, with the most pleasant garden, and most beautiful palace in the world: If contraries illustrate, and the place can admit of any illustration, it must needs add to the splendour of the situation, and to the beauty of the building, and I must say (with which I will close my short observation) if there is any wonder in Chatsworth, it is, that any man who had a genius suitable to so magnificent a design, who could lay out the plan for such a house, and had a fund to support the charge, would built it in such a place where the mountains insult the clouds, intercept the sun, and would threaten, were earthquakes frequent here, to bury the very towns, much more the house, in their ruins.

The remaining article, and which, I grant, we may justly call a WONDER, is Elden Hole: The description of it, in brief, is thus: In the middle of a plain open field, gently descending to the south, there is a frightful chasme, or opening in the earth, or rather in the rock, for the country seems thereabouts to be all but one great rock; this opening goes directly down perpendicular into the earth, and perhaps to the center; it may be twenty foot over one way, and fifty or sixty the other; it has no bottom, that is to say, none that can yet be heard of.

Eldon Hole was finally descended by John Lloyd in 1770 who found it was not bottomless after all, and measured its depth as about 315 feet (96m).

Mr Cotton says, he let down eight hundred fathoms of line into it, and that the plummet drew still; so that, in a word, he sounded about a mile perpendicular; for as we call a mile 1,760 yards, and 884 is above half, then doubtless eight hundred fathoms must be 1,600 yards, which is near a mile.

As Celia Fiennes had suspected, and as Defoe would no doubt have loved to have learned, evidently Cotton's mile-long line must have just coiled up at the bottom of the shaft.

This I allow to be a wonder, and what the like of is not to be found in the world, that I have heard of, or believe. And would former writers have been contented with one wonder instead of seven, it would have done more honour to the Peak, and even to the whole nation, than adding five imaginary miracles to it that had nothing in them, and which really depreciated the whole.

What Nature meant in leaving this window open into the infernal world, if the place lies that way, we cannot tell: But it must be said, there is something of horror upon the very imagination, when one does but look into it; and therefore tho' I cannot find much in Mr. Cotton, of merry memory, worth quoting, yet on this subject, I think, he has four very good lines, speaking of his having an involuntary horror at looking into this pit.

Defoe concludes his account of his visit to the Peak and Derbyshire with a summary of his findings of what he dubbed the 'so-called' Wonders of the Peak.

Having then viewed these things with an impartial mind, give me leave to reduce the wonders of the Peak to a less number, and of a quite different kind.

1. Elden Hole I acknowledge to be a wonderful place, as I have said above; but to me the greatest surprise is, that, after such a real wonder, any of the trifles added to it could bear the name of wonders.

2. Of Buxton; the wonder is to me, that in a nation so full of chronical diseases as we are, such as our scorbuticks, rheumaticks, cholicks, and niphriticks, there should be such a fountain of medicine sent from heaven, and no more notice taken of it, or care to make it useful.

3. That in a nation so curious, so inquiring, and so critical as this, any thing so unsatisfying, so foolish and so weak, should pass for wonders as those of Mam Tor, Tideswell, Poole's Hole &c.

4. As to Chatsworth, the wonder, as I said before, seems to me; not that so noble and magnificent a palace should be built, but that it should be built in such a situation, and in such a country so out of the way, so concealed from the world, that whoever sees it must take a journey on purpose.

The River Derwent at Chatsworth

2.
THE FIRST TOURISTS

The success of Hobbes and Cotton's Seven Wonders gave rise to the discovery of the Peak by the first tourists, many of whom who used the newly developed railway network to get to Derbyshire. They were also encouraged by authors such as William Adam, Ebenezer Rhodes and Ebenezer Elliott, who had produced their own accounts of the wonders of the Peak District, often in lurid and flowery poetry and prose.

Carl Philip Moritz, a German actor and philosopher from the Pied Piper town of Hamelin, published the first edition of his Reisen eines Deutchen in England im Jahr 1782 *(*Journeys of a German in England in 1782*) in 1783, and a second edition appeared in 1785. When it was published for the first time in English in 1795, the translation was said to be the work of an English lady, and it shows an England in the throes of the Enclosure Movement, a scene quite unlike Moritz's homeland in Germany.*

CARL PHILIP MORITZ *Journeys of a German in England in 1782* (1783)

The air was mild and I was cheerful and contented. Then towards midday I had my first view of the romantic scenery of that part of Derbyshire into which I proposed to go. I came to a great height from which I saw at once the whole prospect of these hills before me. Hills near by were succeeded by hill behind them and these in turn were succeeded by others peering through the spaces in between.

Soon I was passing over these – up and down as if on a series of waves. At one moment I was taking in the joy of a wide prospect and at the next I was dipping into a deep hollow.

I had now definitely decided that my goal was to be the great cave at Castleton, in the High Peak of Derbyshire. This was only twenty miles from Matlock.

The earth looked very different here from what I had seen at Windsor and Richmond. Instead of green fields and gentle hills I now saw bare mountains and crags set off against the sky. Instead of green hedges round the fields, they were here enclosed with grey stone walls, and the houses, too, were of this same material, all locally quarried, in a similar traditional style of rough-hewn stones laid almost undressed one upon another in the shape of four walls. One could build such a house with little exertion.

The situation at Matlock itself surpassed all I had expected of it. On the right were several elegant houses for those taking treatment for their ailments at the baths. Smaller cottages hung on the rocks like nests. On the left ran the river [the Derwent] in a deep ravine, almost hidden from sight under a high majestic arch of overhanging trees. A huge stone wall stretched for more than a mile along by this river and secluded paths wound in and out among the shady bushes.

When I came to Matlock I had just got to the description of Paradise in my reading of Milton's *Paradise Lost*, and the following lines, which I read in the ravine by the bank of the river, had a strong effect on my mind, for they describe the nature of the scene as clearly as if the poet had drawn on this very spot for his idea:

> . . . delicious Paradise,
> Now nearer, crowns with her enclosure green,
> As with a rural mound, the champion head
> Of a steep wilderness, whose hairy sides
> With thicket overgrown, grotesque and wild,
> Access denied; . . .

From Matlock Bath a bridge gives access to the town of Matlock itself, which consists of no more than a few ramshackle houses and can hardly be called a village. There is a great deal of traffic here – on horseback and by carriages – because of the proximity of the baths.

From Matlock I went by way of several villages to a little town called Bakewell in a hilly and romantic countryside. Often I made my way by narrow mountain tracks at astonishing heights, seeing a few small cottages nestling deep down in the dale beneath. The grey stone walls that bounded the fields gave the whole district a wild aspect. The hills were mostly bare of trees and in the distance one could see herds feeding on their summits.

As I was passing through one village I heard a big country lad asking another if I was a Frenchman. It seemed he had been waiting a long time to see this wonder and his wish had now been granted.

When I had passed through Bakewell, which is like Derby inasmuch as it is rather unimposing, my path ran by a fairly wide river and over a little mound where a cultivated field lay spread before me, making an indescribably gratifying impression on me. For this I could not account at once, but then I remembered that in my childhood I had seen a place almost identical to this near the village where I was brought up.

And although I was now in the middle of England the field was not enclosed by hedges, but open, as in Germany. It shone with an uninterrupted succession of greens and yellows – a most attractive colouring. This, and the thousand other small details of the scene which I can't enumerate, brought back to me the memory of my childhood.

I rested here, a mile outside Bakewell . . . After my rest by the river I passed through another small place called Ashford. I wanted to reach a little village named Wardlow that evening and it lay only three miles away. But two men whom I had seen in Matlock came into view and shouted at me from a distance to wait for them. These were the first fellow-walkers who had offered to go along with me since I left . . . Oxford.

The first was a saddler who wore a short brown jacket, an apron and a round hat. The other was a very quiet man dressed like a simple townsman – quite unlike the talkative saddler.

I pricked up my ears as I heard the saddler begin to speak of the works of Homer, Horace and Virgil. He quoted lines from their works, moreover, in a way I should have thought only possible in a doctor or master of arts from Oxford. He advised me not to stop at Wardlow, where I should find only mean accommodation, but to go on with him another couple of miles to Tideswell where he lived. This name 'Tideswell' he pronounced 'Tidsel', just as the common people of Birmingham call their town 'Brummagem'.

We called at a little alehouse along the road where the saddler insisted on paying for my drink because he said he had taken me with him along the road.

Not far from this alehouse we came to a hill with a view which, my philosophic saddler said, may possibly be the only one of its kind in England. We saw beneath us a deep hollow, like a cauldron cut out of the surrounding earth, and at its foot a small valley containing a house beside a little stream meandering through a carpet of green pastureland. The man who lived in this happy valley was a great naturalist who, following his bent as a scientist, had already transplanted there a great number of foreign plants. My escort expounded on the beauty of this valley in terms well-nigh poetical, while the third man, bored with his long harangue, grew resentful at the delay.

This was Monsal Head, one of the most popular and most photographed viewpoints in the Peak even today. Moritz, of course, was seeing it some eighty years before the Midland Railway was blasted through it in the 1860s, and without the now iconic, five-arched Monsal Head Viaduct.

A steep path led us down into the valley. We passed through and emerged on the other side between the mountains.

Not far from Tideswell we lost our third companion, who lived thereabouts. Now we could see Tideswell before us.... Tideswell consists of two rows of small houses built of undressed stone. On entering the place my guide drew my attention to the church – very handsome and in modern taste despite its antiquity.

This was the splendid, fourteenth-century Perpendicular parish church of St John the Baptist, Tideswell – the so-called 'Cathedral of the Peak'.

He asked me whether he should take me to a high-class or a homely inn. I chose the latter and so he went with me to a small inn where he introduced me to the landlord as his travelling companion and a man of good perception.

They made their best endeavour to treat me as such, and prepared toasted cheese for me. This was Cheshire cheese toasted before the fire until it was melted. It is regarded as a right delicious dish, and unfortunately I couldn't eat any of it and invited my host to eat it. He enjoyed it as a rare treat. Then, as I drank neither brandy nor ale, he said I lived far too frugally for a walker, who must after all have enough strength to get along.

A man whom I gave sixpence showed me the way out of the town and put me on the right road for Castleton. This road went along by a wall of piled-up stones such I have already described. The whole district was rough and mountainous; the earth brought forth brown heather; here and there a sheep grazed. I made a short digression to a hill on the left, where I saw an awe-inspiring view of bare rocky mountains, beautiful in their way, stretching both near and far; the most distinguished bore black heather and presented a terrible aspect.

THE DEVIL'S CAVERN

I had now left London a hundred and seventy miles behind me. Ascending then one of the highest hills that I had for some time seen before me I saw a thrilling sight. A valley interwoven with rivulets and surrounded by a ring of mountains lay spread out before me. In this valley lay Castleton, a little town of simple houses taking its name from an old castle, the ruins of which are still there to be seen (Peveril Castle).

A narrow path winds down the side of the hill, which led me through the valley and right into a Castleton street where I found a hostelry and dined. Immediately I had done this I set off for the cavern (Peak Cavern). A little brook which flows through the town led me to its entrance.

For a while I stood staring in wonderment at the astounding height of the cliff which rose before me. On both its sides grew green bushes, while above it rose the crumbling walls and towers of the old castle. Beneath me at the foot of the cliff gaped the huge opening of the cave's entrance, pitch-dark as first first in the glare of the midday sun.

As I stood wondering at all this I noticed a man in the gloomy entrance to the cave. His aspect was wild, and when he asked me if I wanted to see the cave his harsh voice echoed loudly from its depths.

I answered him in the affirmative, whereupon he asked me another question. Did I wish to be carried across the stream? He mentioned the fee for this. It was quite small.

His stringy black hair, dirty ragged clothes, his harsh voice and the question he asked were so fitting to the character of Charon that I could not shake off the uncanny feeling that the sight of the cave had begin to inspire.

As soon as I had agreed to his demand he told me to follow him fearlessly, and together we passed into the cave. In its entrance and on my left lay a huge tree-trunk on which the local boys were playing. Our path sloped gradually downwards and the daylight, entering only through the mouth of the cave, was left behind. We were enwrapped in twilight. And when we had gone a few steps forward, what a sight I saw! Glancing to my right I caught sight of a complete village under the huge wall of the cavern! As it was Sunday the inhabitants had a day off from their work and were sitting before their huts with their children. Hardly had we left these little dwellings behind us than I came upon a lot of big wheels, used by the subterranean villagers for the making of ropes. It was as if I were gazing upon the wheel of Ixion and the interminable labour of the Danaides.

As we went farther down into the cave the twilight deepened as the receding opening of the cave seemed to get smaller and smaller, until but a few rays of light reached us through the smoke, that twisted up into the vault. This gradual closing in of darkness as you go down the steady incline inspires a soft melancholy; the threat of life is, as it were, being snipped off without any pain or grief and one wanders serenely to the peaceful land where there is no more care.

After Moritz's exploration of Peak Cavern (he paid 2s 6d – 12½p – for the trip, tipping his guide 'because he received none of the official fee, but had to hand it all over to his master; who lived very comfortably on the income from his cavern, keeping an underling to show the people round'), his shoes were in need of mending, and the shoemaker, 'a master craftsman', offered to take him to see Mam Tor, 'one of the wonders of Nature in Derbyshire'.

This mountain is covered with turf on its back and sides, but at one end forms a steep precipice. The body of this mountain, however, is not of hard rock like the other mountains, but consists of loose earth (shale) which breaks away and either trickles downward in small quantities or collapses in great lumps which roll down with a noise

The 'Shivering Mountain' of Mam Tor, from Odin Mine, Castleton

like thunder. These fallen quantities of earth pile up at the foot of the mountain and in this way are building up a smaller hill which continually grows higher.

It seems probable that the name of this mountain – Mam Tor – comes from this phenomenon and means 'Mother tor' (or mountain); for 'tor' is an abbreviation of 'tower', meaning the height, while 'mam' is a common abbreviation of 'mother'. The mountain is creating a hill at its foot and is therefore its mother. There is a belief among local inhabitants that the mountain still remains the same size notwithstanding the daily loss of material from its body.

Not far from this point is the Eldon Hole – a hole in the ground of such enormous depth that if you throw a pebble down it and lay your ear to the ground at its rim you can hear the pebble falling for a long time. All the time it is falling you hear remarkable sounds. First, with the release of the pebble, a sound like a sigh, then, as the pebble strikes against the hard sides of the hole on its descent, oscillating to and fro, a rumble like subterranean thunder, until, after a long time falling it reaches the bottom and the noise suddenly ends in a hiss.

The credulous folk hereabouts firmly believe that one of them once threw a goose into this hole and that it reappeared two miles away in the Great Peak Cavern I have described, completely featherless. They believe other fairy-tales of the same order.

In Derbyshire they tell of the Seven Wonders of Nature, of which this Eldon Hole is one; another is Mam Tor and a third the Great Peak Cavern which goes locally by the rather dirty name of 'The Devil's Arse'.

I have brought with me from the cave a cough which I don't like at all. It gives me much pain and I think one is forced to breathe damp air in that cavern; but in that case how has Sharon stuck it so long?

This morning I rose early in order to see the ruined castle [Peveril Castle] and to climb the very high hill adjacent.

The ruins stand right over the mouth of the cave, on a hill which extends well beyond the ruins, getting ever broader, but in the front is so narrow that the castle wall occupies all this part of the hill. Downwards from the castle it is all steep rock, so there is no access to it from the town except by a path hewn out of the rock, and that is very steep.

The ruins stand on a spot all overgrown with nettles and thistles. Formerly there would be a bridge joining one cliff with another opposite; some traces remain, for in the valley beneath can be found the remains of the arch which once supported the bridge. This valley, which lies behind the ruins and probably over the Great Peak Cavern, is called Caves Way

[Cave Dale] and is one of the main roads into the town. It begins very gently in the distance and descends between the two mountains on a course by no means tiring, but if you miss this course and continue over the hill, you will be in great danger of falling from the cliff as it gets steeper all the time.

The mountain on which the ruins stand is completely rocky, but the other – on the left of it across the vale – is grass-grown, with the pastures on its summit separated by undressed stone walls. This green hill is at least three times as high as that on which the ruins stand [Moritz appears to be referring to Cow Low].

I started to climb the green hill. This is rather steep and when I got just over halfway up without looking round I found myself in much the same situation as the man who had climbed Mam Tor for a wager. I found on looking back that I had no head for heights; the sight of the land lying like a map beneath me almost unnerved me; the roofs of the houses seemed to be almost on the ground and the castle mound itself lay at my feet.

I grew giddy at this sight and had to use all my reason to prove to myself that I was in no danger; in any case I could scramble down the green turf in the same way as I had come up it. But in time I grew accustomed to the view until at last it gave me real satisfaction. I climbed to the summit, walked across the pastures and came at last to the road which brought me gently through the valley between two mountains.

Above me in the pasture on the mountain some milk-maids had been milking their cows and were now returning down this road with their milking-pails on their heads. It was beautiful to see a group of these girls, taking shelter beneath an overhanging rock, chatting confidentially to each other as they sat on natural seats formed by the stones.

At this stage I must remind you that the word 'peak' generally means the tip of a mountain, but 'The Peak' or 'High Peak' of Derbyshire, as many say, is the mountainous or highest part of that county.

Ebenezer Rhodes (1762–1839) was a Rotherham-born former master cutler, perhaps better known as a topographer, publisher and artist. He published the first part of his folio edition of his Peak Scenery, or the Derbyshire Tourist, *dedicated to the Duke of Devonshire and illustrated by Francis Chantrey, in 1818.*

EBENEZER RHODES *Peak Scenery, or the Derbyshire Tourist* (1818)

That part of Derbyshire known by the name of the HIGH PEAK, is every where composed of a succession of hills, of a greater or lesser elevation, and intervening dales, which play into each other in various directions. Throughout the whole the same general character prevails. A thin mossy verdure, often intermingled with grey barren rock, adorns their sides; and sometimes the interference of what Mr Farey has denominated '*indestructible lime-stone Rubble*', disfigures their steep acclivities. Yet even then a little brush-wood occasionally breaks in to enliven and diversify the otherwise sterile scene. These remarks particularly apply to the minor dales of Derbyshire. Those which form the channels of the principal rivers are of a more elevated description, and possess, in an eminent degree, that variety of object, form, and colour, which is essential to picturesque beauty, sometimes united with a magnitude of parts where grandeur and sublimity preside in solitary stillness.

Travellers accustomed to well wooded and highly cultivated scenes only, have frequently expressed a feeling bordering on disgust, at the bleak and barren appearance of the mountains in the Peak of Derbyshire; but to the man whose taste is unsophisticated by a fondness for artificial adornments, they possess superior interest, and impart more pleasing sensations. Remotely seen, they are often beautiful; many of their forms, even when near, are decidedly good; and in distance the features of rudeness, by which they are occasionally marked, are softened down to general and harmonious masses. The graceful and long-continued outline which they present, the breadth of light and shadow that spreads over their extended surfaces, and the delightful colouring with which they are sometimes invested, never fails to attract the attention of the picturesque traveller. But there are persons who, unfortunately for themselves, cannot easily be pleased with what they see; and who, like Sterne's Smelfungus, can 'travel from Dan to Beersheba, and cry – 'tis all barren'.

Inland landscape may likewise (as with coastal scenery) derive an accession of picturesque effect from the incidental intervention of mists and clouds, for nature has a thousand ways of enriching the many views he has spread before us. These shadowy nothings, these thin and evanescent visitants, not only serve to vary and diversify the scene, but in a mountainous country they are, occasionally, the source of considerable beauty. To trace the white clouds floating across the bosom of the hills of Derbyshire, their highest peak sometimes illuminated with a bright sunny ray, and sometimes compassed around with the majesty of darkness, is at least an amusing, if not a sublime employment: it calls into play the reveries of imagination, a faculty which is always more delightful with objects of its own creation, than with what it finds definitively formed and incapable of its arbitrary modifications.

Such are the appearances that often occur amongst the mountains of Derbyshire. Descending into the dales, especially those through which the Derwent, the Dove, and the Wye meander, the eye is enchanted with brilliant streams, well cultivated meadows, luxuriant foliage, steep heathy hills, and craggy rocks, which administer to the delight of the traveller, and alternately sooth or elevate his mind as he moves along.

Travellers on the A6 between Matlock and Bakewell might note a solitary sycamore atop a small hill to the left as they approach the one-street village of Darley Dale. The tradition attached to this singular landmark was the subject of a poem by William Wordsworth, who also wrote in praise of the palatial home of the Dukes of Devonshire, Chatsworth.

WILLIAM WORDSWORTH *A Tradition of Oker Hill in Darley Dale, Derbyshire* (1829)

'Tis said that to the brow of yon fair hill
Two brothers clomb, and, turning face from face,
Nor one look more exchanging, grief to still
Or feed, each planted on that lofty place
A chosen Tree; then, eager to fulfil
Their courses, like two new-born rivers, they
In opposite directions urged their way
Down from the far-seen mount. No blast might kill
Or blight that fond memorial; – the trees grew,
And now entwine their arms; but ne'er again

Embraced those Brothers upon earth's wide plain;
Nor aught of mutual joy or sorrow knew
Until their spirits mingled in the sea
That to itself takes all, Eternity.

WILLIAM WORDSWORTH 'Chatsworth' (1835)

CHATSWORTH! thy stately mansion, and the pride
Of thy domain, strange contrast do present
To house and home in many a craggy rent
Of the wild Peak; where new-born waters glide
Through fields those thrifty occupants abide
As in a dear and chosen banishment,
With every semblance of entire content;
So kind is simple Nature, fairly tried!
Yet He whose heart in childhood gave her troth
To pastoral dales, thin-set with modest farms,
May learn, if judgement strengthen with his growth,
That, not for Fancy only, pomp hath charms;
And, strenuous to protect from lawless harms
The extremes of favoured life, may honour both.

The following is a typically over-the-top excerpt from the effusive pen of Ebenezer Elliott, the Sheffield-based 'Corn Law Rhymer' – entitled Win-Hill: Or the Curse of God, *which was written after witnessing a storm when climbing Win Hill in the Hope Valley.*

EBENEZER ELLIOTT *Win-Hill: Or the Curse of God* (1835)

How wildly start the wild flocks as we gaze!
How softly sleeps upon the lap of noon
The cloud-couch'd lightning! And how sweetly plays
The laughing blue above the blackness; soon
To melt in fire and horror, where, aboon
This lesser giant's storm-swoll'n floods and firs,
Yon distant giant fronts the mid-day moon,
While solemnly the wind-fed wigan [rowan or mountain ash] stirs
Its flapping leaves alone, o'er fern and sun-bright furze!

To bathe with married waves their monarch's feet,
See, where the Ashop and the Derwent haste;
And how he rears him from the vale, complete
In all his time-touch'd majesty, embraced
By the blue, bright blue heavens; his proud brow graced
With that stone diadem with Nature made,
Ages before her practised hand had graced
With living gems the bluebell-haunted shade;
Or, high in lucid air, her wind-swift wings display'd!

King of the Peak! Win-Hill! thou throned and crowned,
That reign'st o'er many a stream, and many a vale!
Star-loved, and meteor-sought, and tempest-found!
Proud centre of a mountain-circle, hail!
But, Eldest Brother of the Air and Light,
Firm shalt thou stand when demigods turn pale!
For thou, ere Science dawned on Reason's night
Wast, and wilt be when Mind shall rule all other might.

The summit of Win Hill, showing the Ladybower Reservoir

To be a crown'd and sceptred curse, that makes
Immortal worms! A wolf, that feeds on souls!
One of the names which vengeance whips with snakes,
Whose venom cannot die! A king of ghouls,
Whose drink is blood! To be clear-eyed as owls,
To be a tiger-king, whose mercy growls!
To be of meanest things the vilest thing!
Throned asp o'er lesser asps! What grub would be a king!

But crown'ed Win-Hill! To be a king like thee!
Older than death! As God's thy calm behest!
Calling the feeble to thy sheltering breast,
And shaking beauty from they gorgeous vest,
And loved by every good and happy thing!

With nought beneath thee that thos hast not bless'd,
And nought above thee but the Almighty's wing!
O glorious god-like aim! Who would not be a king?

But, lo, the Inn! The mountain-girded Inn!
Whose amber stream is worth all Helicon!
To pass it fasting were a shame and sin;
Stop! For the gate hangs well that hinders none;
Refresh, and pay, then stoutly travel on!
Ay, thou hast need to pree the barley-wine;
Steep is the ascent, O bard! thou look'st upon;
To reach that cloud-capt seat, and throne divine,
Might try a stronger frame and younger limbs than thine.

No, having drunk of jolly ale enough,
To climb Win-Hill is worth ambition – yea!
Ambition, e'en if made of jolly stuff,
Should drink strong ale, or never will he say
To rival climbers – 'Follow on my way!'
Old ale and jolly, be it dark or pale,
Drink like a toper, be thou green or grey!
Drink oft and long, or try to climb, and fail!
If thou would'st climb Win-Hill, drink old and jolly ale!

'Blow, blow, thou breeze of mountain freshness, blow!'
Stronger and fresher still, as we ascend
Strengthen'd and freshen'd, till the land below
Lies like a map! – On! on! Those clouds portend
Hail, rain, and fire! – Hark, how the rivers send
Their skyward voices hither, and their words

Of liquid music! – See, how bluely blend
The east moors with the sky! – The lowing herds,
To us, are silent now, and hush'd the songful birds.

High on the topmost jewel of thy crown,
Win-Hill! I sit bareheaded, ankle-deep,
In tufts of rose-cupped bilberries; and look down
On towns that smoke below, and homes that creep
Into the silvery clouds, which far-off keep
Their sultry state! and many a mountain stream
And many a mountain vale, 'and ridgy steep';
The Peak, and all his mountains where they gleam
Or frown, remote or near, more distant than they seem!

There flows the Ashop, yonder bounds the Wye,
And Derwent here towards princely Chatsworth trends;
But while the Nough [Noe] steals purple from the sky,
Lo, northward far, what giants' shadow bends?
A voice of torrents, hark! its wailing sends!
Who drives yon tortured cloud through still-stone air?
A rush! a roar! a wing, a whirlwind rends
The stooping larch. The moorlands cry 'Prepare!
'It comes! ye gore-gorged foes of want and toil, beware!'

It comes! Behold! – Black Blakelow [Bleaklow] hoists on high
His signals to the blast from Gledhill's [Glead Hill's] brow.
Then, slowing glooming on the lessing sky,
The bread-tax's exile sees, (in speechless woe,

Wandering the melancholy main below,
Where round the shores of Man the dark surge heaves,)
And while his children's tears in silence flow,
Thinks of sweet scenes, to which his sould still cleaves,
That home on Etherow's side, which he for ever leaves.

Now expectation listens, mute and pale,
While, ridged with sudden foam, the Derwent brawls,
Arrow-like comes the rain, like the fire the hail.
And hark! Mam Tor on shuddering Stanage calls!
See, what a frown o'er castled Winnats falls!
Down drops the death-black sky! And Kinderscout,
Conscious of glory, laughs at intervals;
Then lifts his helmet, throws his thunder out,
Bathes all the hills in flame, and hails their stormy shout.

William Adam, who dedicated his Gem of the Peak *(1843) to the Duke of Devonshire, was another Victorian writer whose passionate descriptions, to modern eyes at least, are completely over the top. His description of the approach to Chatsworth and also to Dovedale, is typically rhapsodic.*

WILLIAM ADAM *The Gem of the Peak: Matlock Bath and its Vicinity* (1843)

CHATSWORTH

Chatsworth, how can I describe thee! Art thou not a Gem of purest water dug out of the rugged mountains that surround thee, cut and bounded by a thousand *facets* with exquisite skill and admirable taste to set off they native beauties? Surely thou art a very Paradise, again established among the haunts of men, – again adorning our 'nether' world!

> I glanc'd around the 'scene' from right to left,
> It seem'd as Paradise was passing by,
> And I beheld it from a 'secret cleft'.
>
> – Edwards

Reader, if you should be privileged to see Chatsworth on a day when the gleams of a brilliant summer's sun repose in soft and quiet glory on beautiful lawns, adorned with trees of such majesty, studding them in clusters, or forming a thick impenetrable barrier on their outskirts, – swelling eminences, exhibiting the most graceful undulations for miles around you, – the crystal stream here broken up into a series of cascades by rough artificial ledges, and there reflecting the fine objects on either side from its quiet expanse of waters, – the deer of many species, and the lowing cattle tossing their heads aloft and plunging into its midst, or laving their sides as at a cooling fountain, – the water-works throwing up perpetually their *snowy* and shining column as it were to the very heavens, – the noble house, a perfect model of splendid workmanship and taste, on its elegant terrace, with its Indian flower-beds and sweet groves, – its windows, balustrades and battlements gleaming in the sunbeam.

– To behold all this splendour nearly surrounded by a bleak belt of mountains; their rugged and overhanging cliffs towering above it; as if chosen on purpose as a fitting and appropriate *frame*, the better to set off the varied charms and superlative beauties of this exquisite Picture, – then will you not be surprised that we have prefaced our observations on Chatsworth by a kind of rhapsody – for cold and frigid must be the heart which remains unmoved, when, on gently ascending the road over the rising ground in the park, – the lovely pleasure grounds and glorious pile of Chatsworth breaks gradually on the *view like a moving picture*, backed by woods of such magnificence, and shaggy moors of such elevation! – surely combinations like these should kindle in the bosom the noblest sentiments, and excite the best and *purest feelings* of our reverence!

DOVEDALE

There is an indescribable and overpowering majesty in nature, especially in mountain scenery, that is difficult to account for; it seems not so much to arise from a minute examination of the parts of which it is composed, as from the combined effect of the whole as it is rapidly traversed by the eye, until the mind is completely filled with its vast dimensions, and inspired with a deep sense of its own insignificance and nothingness, as compared with such monuments of creative wisdom and omnipotent power; and that power reigning in supreme though silent majesty around us. We experienced the full effect of this as we made our way from the smiling fields and busy haunts of man to plunge into and examine the deep and narrow recesses of Dovedale, which still retains all its ancient simplicity and beauty, uninjured by the art of man, and its magic charm still unbroken by the intrusion of his dwellings. – It would seem, therefore, that its solitude is that which, combined with its romantic scenery, speaks so impressively to the heart, and which has elicited the admiration of all the lovers of nature, and been the theme of their praise from the days of old Izaak Walton to those of Sir Humphrey Davy. Byron, in one of his letters to his friend Moore, asks 'if he had seen Dovedale!' and assures him that 'there are things in Derbyshire as noble as Greece of Switzerland!' In fact, it has been the subject of such repeated observation and remark, that any further description of its beauties might be deemed quite superfluous – and besides, the task is not so easy as at first sight it appears to be, to string together a number of high-sounding epithets about lofty mountains, towering crags, abrupt precipices, and a lovely river flowing smoothly or sometimes fretting and foaming amongst them; but to convey to the mind of a stranger a just conception of the Dale, to lead him through all its sinuosities, pointing out its romantics beauties and ever-changing character of rock and cliff, the rippling stream and the foaming fall, without straining and exciting too much the imagination by a false colouring, and yet to rise to the loftiness and beauty of the subject, is a task of no ordinary difficulty; but we must try, if we fail in the attempt.

Despite these apparent self-inflicted misgivings, Adam goes on to devote seven pages on his effulgent description of the dale.

Dovedale

3.
THE COMING OF THE RAILWAYS

As previously stated, the Victorian 'discovery' of the Peak was undoubtedly facilitated by the coming of the railways, and spas like Matlock Bath (dubbed 'the English Switzerland') and Buxton became fashionable places of resort for tourists and Romantic writers like Wordsworth, Byron and Ruskin. And the first guidebooks appeared, as their authors – such as James Croston and Louis Jennings – ventured into the hills and cashed in on the new-found love of romantic scenery.

Best-selling and much-filmed Victorian novelist Charlotte Brontë often stayed at Hathersage with her friend Ellen Nussey, so knew the surrounding moors very well. She is thought to have based her melodramatic novel on the Eyre family's Tudor tower house of North Lees Hall, which shelters beneath Stanage Edge, above Hathersage. This is an excerpt from Charlotte's best-known novel, Jane Eyre, *as Jane arrives on the moors above Hathersage.*

CHARLOTTE BRONTË *Jane Eyre* (1847)

The roads were heavy, the night misty; my conductor let his horse walk all the way, and the hour and a half extended, I verily believe, to two hours; at last he turned in his seat and said: – 'You're noan so far fro' Thornfield now.'

Again I looked out: we were passing a church; I saw its low broad tower against the sky, and its bell tolling a quarter; I saw a narrow galaxy of lights too, on a hill-side, marking a village or hamlet. About ten minutes after, the driver got down and opened a pair of gates: we passed through, and they clashed to behind us. We slowly ascended a drive, and came upon the long front of a house: candle-light gleamed from one curtained bow-window; all the rest were dark. The car stopped at the front door; it was opened by a maid-servant; I alighted and went in . . .

Next morning, Jane arose and explored Thornfield Hall.

North Lees Hall

Traversing the long and matted gallery, I descended the slippery steps of oak; then I gained the hall: I halted there a minute; I looked at some pictures on the walls (one I remember represented a grim man in a cuirass, and one a lady with powdered hair and a pearl necklace), at a bronze lamp pendent from the ceiling, at a great clock whose case was of oak curiously carved, and ebon black with time and rubbing.

Everything appeared very stately and imposing to me: but then I was so little accustomed to grandeur. The hall-door, which was half of glass, stood open; I stepped over the threshold. It was a fine Autumn morning; the early sun shone serenely on embrowned groves and still green fields: advancing on to the lawn, I looked up and surveyed the front of the mansion. It was three stories high, of proportions not vast, though considerable; a gentleman's manor-house, not a nobleman's seat: battlements round the top gave it a picturesque look. Its grey front stood out well from the back-ground of a rookery, whose cawing tenants were now on the wing: they flew over the lawn and grounds to a light in a great meadow, from which these were separated by a sunk fence, and where an array of mighty old thorn trees, strong, knotty, and broad as oaks, at once explained the etymology of the mansion's designation. Farther off were hills: not so lofty as those round Lowood, nor so craggy, nor so like barriers of separation from the living world; but yet quiet and lonely hills enough, and seeming to embrace Thornfield with a seclusion I had not expected to find existent so near the stirring locality of Millcote. A little hamlet, whose roofs were blent with trees, straggled up the side of one of these hills; the church of the district stood nearer Thornfield: its old tower-top looked over a knoll between the house and gates.

I was yet enjoying the calm prospect and pleasant fresh air, yet listening with delight to the cawing of the rooks, yet surveying the wide, hoary front of the hall, and thinking what a great place it was for one lonely little dame like Mrs. Fairfax to inhabit, when that lady appeared at the door.

Later, as Jane fled Thornfield, the coachman drops her off at Whitcross, which was probably Moscar Cross, off the Glossop Road to the west of Sheffield.

Whitcross is no town, nor even a hamlet; it is but a stone pillar set up where four roads meet: white-washed, I suppose, to be more obvious at a distance and in darkness. Four arms spring from its summit: the nearest town to which these point is, according to the inscription, distant ten miles; the farthest, above twenty. From the well-known names of these towns I learn in what county I have lighted; a north-midland shire, dusk with moorland, ridged with mountain: this I see. There are great moors behind and on each hand of me; there are waves of mountains far beyond that deep valley at my feet. The population here must be thin, and I see no passengers on these roads; they stretch out east, west, north, and south – white, broad, lonely; they are all cut in the moor, and the heather grows deep and wild to their very verge.

George Eliot (Mary Anne Evans) claimed that she used a male pen name to ensure her work would be taken seriously. She said she wanted to escape the stereotype of women only writing lighthearted romances. This excerpt is from her famous novel Adam Bede, *published in 1859. 'Stonyshire' is the novelist's name for Derbyshire and 'Loamshire' is her Staffordshire.*

GEORGE ELIOT *Adam Bede* (1859)

'I like th' hills best,' said Seth, 'when the clouds are over your head, and you see the sun shining ever so far off, over the Loamford way, as I've often done o' late, on the stormy days: it seems to me as if that was heaven where there's always joy and sunshine, though this life's dark and cloudy.'

'Oh, I love the Stonyshire side,' said Dinah; 'I shouldn't like to set my face towards the countries where they're rich in corn and cattle, and the ground so level and easy to tread; and to turn my back on the hills where the poor people have to live such a hard life, and the men spend their days in the mines away from the sunlight. It's very blessed on a bleak cold day, when the sky is

Thorpe Cloud and the Stepping Stones, Dovedale

hanging dark over the hill, to feel the love of God in one's soul, and carry it to the lonely, bare, stone houses, where there's nothing else to give comfort.'

Local authors Eliza Cook and James Croston also waxed lyrical about their native country. James Croston FSA (1830–93) was born in Hulme, Manchester, and was employed as a clerk, and ship and insurance broker. In 1874 he was living at Upton Hall, Prestbury, near Macclesfield, and wrote the historical and topographical descriptions for Francis Chantrey's Peak Scenery, or Views in Derbyshire *(1889).*

ELIZA COOK *Derbyshire Dales* (n.d.)

Sweet pass of the 'Dove'! mid rock, river and dingle,
How great is thy charm for the wanderer's breast!
With thy moss-girdled towers and foam-jewelled shingle
Thy mountains of might, and thy valleys of rest.
Wild glen of dark 'Taddington' – rich in thy robing
Of forest-green cloak, with grey lacing bedight;
How I lingered to watch the red Western rays probing
Thy leaf-mantled bosum with lanes of light!

And 'Monsal', thou mine of Arcadian treasure,
Need we seek for 'Greek Islands' and spice-laden gales,
While a Temple like thee of enchantment and pleasure
May be found in our own Derbyshire Dales?

JAMES CROSTON *On Foot through the Peak* (1st edition, 1868)

But he who would thoroughly appreciate the rich stores of England's beauty must leave her iron roads and beaten highways and wander lovingly over her green hills, and explore the mazy windings of her secluded dales – in the early greyness of the morning, when the mists linger in the vales, and the dew lies heavy upon the grass – at mid-day, when the landscape is bathed in brilliant sunlight – and at eventide, when the declining sun fills the glowing west with gorgeous beauty, when the shadows lie in lengthened lines upon the grassy slopes, and the woods and valleys are wrapped in the rich glow of golden light. He must follow the sweet meanderings of her mountain streams, winding hither and thither through shady nooks, fringed and festooned with greenery, where the tributary rills come trickling down from the mossy heights, gladdening the ear with their tiny melodies. He must loiter in her by-lanes, between banks rife with ferns, foxgloves, and blooming harebells, where the thick hedgerows and the nodding trees mingle and form a bower overhead, and the bright sunbeams, playing through the leaves, dapple the greensward with their restless and ever-changing shadows. And so pace from hamlet to hamlet, and from village to village, inhaling the fragrance of the flowery meads, and listening to the joyous warblings of the birds, the mingled harmony of dancing leaves, the lowing of the kine, and the gentle murmuring of sunny music. If he will do all this, he will understand something of the charms of English scenery, and will learn that travelling at home is not less enjoyable than travelling abroad.

How much enjoyment may be derived from things that seem trifling in themselves! The naked lifeless-looking rock – the shattered crag – the fragment of limestone with its conglomerate of primeval shells – even the tiny pebble that we kick before us – all bear some evidence of the inner life of nature, and reveal something of the history of a pre-Adamite or an antediluvian age, showing how worlds are constructed upon the wreck and ruin of preceding worlds. And how closely the waxing and waning of living races are bound up and associated with each other.

We know of no district that better repays investigation than the Peak of Derbyshire, and to those in search of novel and rational sources of amusement, or who desire to cultivate a more intimate acquaintance with the charms of nature, there are few that offer a greater fund of exciting interest, or to which an excursion can be made with more pleasurable results.

With us Derbyshire has long been a favourite theme. On its moorland wastes our first lessons in peripatetics were learned. We have scaled its loftiest hills and explored the labyrinthine passages of its cavernous recesses; we have admired the wild scenery of its bleak moors and the charming beauty of its pastoral vales; we have roamed with delight over its heathery heights and plucked the wild flowers in its secluded dells; we have looked down upon the sweet vale of Castleton, and viewed the still more beautiful Hope Dale, from the brow of Mam Tor; with light and cheerful step we have climbed the steep acclivities of the rock, from the verge of which, for centuries past, the great stronghold of the Peverels has frowned upon the vale below –

> The fierce and haughty Peverel's tower,
> The tower which Scott hath hallowed by romance,
> Standing in ruin on its lofty cliff.

The following is an account of a walk taken by Louis John Jennings (1836–93), a Times *journalist and Conservative politician, from the Snake Inn towards Fairbrook Naze, in the days when such excursions were uncommon, and frowned on by the moorland owners who jealously guarded these hills for their grouse shooting. Born in Walworth, London, Jennings later edited the* New York Times *after he moved to America. Jennings returned to London in 1876 and became MP for Stockport. He wrote several outdoor books, including ones on walks in Sussex and Surrey as well as the Peak District.*

LOUIS J. JENNINGS *Rambles Among the Hills* (1880)

Four or five miles from Ashopton the scenery begins to give the traveller an idea of what the Peak is actually like. There are no longer even sheep to be seen on the hills, and the frequent watercourses and spongy nature of the soil render wandering over them slow and difficult work. The mountains are broken up into huge shoulders, with streams running between many of them, deep in heather and ferns, and of a very dark colour owing to the peaty water which trickles over the surface, or stands in deep pools. After a seven miles' walk, I came to the 'Snake Inn', on the edge of the sternest part of the scenery. After a slight rest, I returned to a brook which I had passed on the road, crossed the bridge . . . and followed the stream up for a long distance towards Fairbrook Naze. The track ran over the hills, amid heather and ferns, exceeding all other paths I had yet encountered in savage beauty. Vain would it be to try to describe the scene as I advanced farther and farther towards the mystic region left blank upon the Ordnance Survey map, a region of which a large part is very rarely traversed by human foot. There is a mass of stern and lonely hills, many of them with rounded tops, and beyond them again is a wild and trackless waste of moss and heath and bog, intersected by deep runnels of water, soft and spongy to the tread, and dotted here and there with treacherous moss. So strange, so wild, so desolate a region it would be hard to find elsewhere in England, unless, perhaps, we are to liken Dartmoor to it.

Defoe, in a work now seldom opened, *A Tour through the whole Island of Great Britain*, makes a passing reference to this little-known tract, although he did not visit it. 'This, perhaps,' he says, 'is the most desolate, wild, and abandoned country in all England. The Mountains of the Peak of which I have been speaking seem to be but the beginning of Mountains, or, if you will, as the Lower Rounds of a Ladder.' There was, indeed, a somewhat forbidding aspect over this dark, weird, apparently impenetrable fastness, this

> wild abyss,
> The womb of Nature, and perhaps her grave.

Yet it also had a strange fascination with it, and it was only when the twilight began to close in, casting blacker shadows than before over this domain of 'chaos and old night', that I reluctantly began to retrace my steps down little platforms in miniature cascades. Sometimes a track made by the sheep runs on the side of the hills; sometimes there is no track at all, and one has to follow the brook as best one may. As I emerged from this labyrinth of hills, the darkness rapidly came on, and I was startled by seeing a fire on the other side of the road, with shadowy figures flitting before it.

Another taste of the 'bad old days' when access to Kinder was strictly limited and needed a pass from one of the many landowners. Jennings gives a fine description of negotiating the hags and groughs of the summit plateau of Kinder Scout, and of a disappointing visit to Kinder Downfall.

THE KINDERSCOUT

The first discovery which my inquiries brought to light was that the Kinderscout is regarded as strictly private property, and that it is divided up among numerous holders, almost all of whom are at loggerheads with each other and with the public. The mountain – for one may so speak of it, seeing that it is close upon 2,000 feet in height – is one vast moor, intersected with long, broad gulches, and abounding in deep holes, patches of wet moss, and pools of dark water. There are said to be certain public rights of foot-way, but they do not appear to lead to the best points, and even in regard to these there are constant disputes. Moreover, they are hard to find amidst a labyrinth of heath and ferns, and it is not unusual for the gamekeepers to turn strangers back even when they are upon the paths which are supposed to be fairly open to all. The owners of the moor are jealous to the last degree of their rights, and quarrel over the few birds which by some accident are still left as though the cause of empire were at stake. This arises from the foolish way in which the district has been parcelled out among a number of small holders, in patches not much larger than a table-cloth. One man's allotment is actually under two acres in extent, and his only chance of getting a shot is on the days when his neighbours are out shooting, and the grouse are driven over his field. Then he stands waiting for a chance, and if he can manage to bring a bird down on his little patch, he has had a fine day's sport, but if the bird drops outside his boundary, he goes home with an empty bag.

The stranger in these parts would naturally pay very little heed to local troubles and bickerings if he did not speedily find that they materially interfered with his freedom. If you go to the right you are liable to be warned off; if to the left, to be threatened with an action for trespass. You get permission from three or four different holders, and find that there is still another who bars the way. While mentioning these facts, however, I am bound to add that personally I experienced no inconvenience whatever. The gentlemen of the district not only placed their information at my disposal in a most obliging manner, although I was entirely unknown to them, but gave me permission to go where I pleased. Here, as everywhere else, the stranger will meet with all civility if he begins by himself showing it to others. But people who insist on going everywhere without so much as a 'by your leave', and who delight in fussing and flourishing about, and butting their conceited heads against local prejudices, ought not to go to the Kinderscout; and indeed it is a pity they do not stay at home altogether.

The view from above Hollinhead, on the side of Mill Hill, is another memorable one . . . to the left is the fine point of the Scout called Kinder Low End. From thence the eye can wander gradually round to the Fall, with its precipitous sides and its wild drift of stones, over which dark storm-clouds lower even when the sun shines in the valley far beyond. There is, of course, no road now – all is dark moor, relieved here and there in colour by patches of a soft and beautiful green, tempting the traveller to leave his rough climbing and go and walk upon them. But enticing as they are they must be avoided, for they are ankle-deep or waist-deep in water, according to the rain that may have recently fallen. Immense rocks and boulders are strewn over the surface of Mill Hill, many of them half-covered with heather, and having deep holes at their sides into which the unwary foot is almost sure to slip. The stranger cannot to too cautious in plodding his way over this rugged region, especially if he happens to be alone; for a sprained ankle would be quite sufficient to put him to considerable inconvenience in a spot not visited perhaps for weeks together.

Leaving the most broken part of Mill Hill a little to the left, and gradually working my way up to the top, I saw below me a pool of water high above the valley. The sun had come out for a few moments, and the blue sky above the mountain pool made it gleam like a sapphire. This is called the Mermaid's Pool, and they say that at twelve o'clock at night, as Easter Sunday is coming in, if you go and look steadily into that pool you will see a mermaid. It is worth trying, for surely we should all like to see a genuine mermaid, especially if they are as pretty as the pictures make them; but Easter Sunday had come and gone when I was there. Nevertheless, even without the mermaid, the pool shone out like a beautiful gem amid so much that was dark and gloomy in aspect.

A few grouse had evidently chosen the moor near the pool as their favourite abode, and called to each other with their strange guttural cry, like the two words, 'Go back! Go back!' And there are times when the warning ought to be duly heeded by the stranger, but it was not one of them on the day I am describing, and therefore I left the cock grouse to be wrangled over by his numerous owners, and in course of time found myself at the top of the hill, and kept pretty close to the edge of it in an easterly direction.

The rocks are exactly like sea-cliffs, sometimes very precipitous, and defying any kind of vegetation to take root among them for some distance down. At times they are placed one upon another in thin layers; at others they stand out in vast masses, hanging over the edge of the mountain on so slender a foundation that it seems as if the slightest touch would push them over. At the top of the mountain, the walking is far more difficult than on the sides.

Now begin the deep trenches, the long winding watercourses with sandy bottoms, the dangerous holes thinly covered over with heather, the green oases in this sterile land, which the traveller will touch only to his sorrow and dismay. You go along a yard or two and come to a yawning ditch, with no water perhaps at the bottom, but with soft peat sides which will scarcely bear your weight. Down you go, and after scrambling to the top, expecting to see a smooth table-land before you, and to find all your troubles over, a long vista of similar ditches stretches away in all directions, few less than four feet in depth, and many of them at least ten. It is tiring work to go in and over them, for as the farmer complained of the claret they do not bring one 'any forrarder' – one makes no perceptible progress. Besides all this, there are long round-about tramps which it is necessary to take to avoid the swamps and bogs, and the occasional wrenches which one is sure to get through slipping down holes.

But the scenery is an ample recompense for all the trouble – a more glorious mountain view there cannot be in England. The hills of Cheshire, the moors on the high ranges above Buxton, line after line stretches far away till sky and mountain meet, and the eye gets bewildered amid so much savage grandeur and so many chaotic forms and outlines.

The Kinder Fall looks like a huge cliff rent violently asunder, strewn on both sides with boulders – at the top a broken mass of stone and rubble, then two comparatively smooth ledges, and then a confused heap of rocks and boulders, which extends far into the valley, sometimes almost blocking it up, so that the stream has to worm its way in and out, or is forced to continue its route in miniature cascades. The water must take its rise partly in springs, for very little was coming over the Kinder Fall on either of the occasions of my visits, although the stream at the bottom was always tolerably full. The traveller will hear stories of the Fall at Hayfield which will lead him to expect very much more than there is for him to see.

John Ruskin was taken to Matlock for the first time by his parents as a boy of ten in 1829, and visited the area himself many times later. This is his description of the landscape which had obviously made a lasting impression on the outstanding Victorian author, critic and conservationist, who also had close connections with the neighbouring city of Sheffield. Ruskin's St George's Guild purchased a 13-acre farm for a group of Sheffield workmen, which was run initially as an allotment scheme, then as a land colony with about twelve members. It is still known as St George's Farm, or the Totley Colony. He recalled the effect that the county had on his childhood in a much-quoted but unpublished letter.

JOHN RUSKIN 'Railways in Derbyshire' (1884)

In its very minuteness it is the most educational of all the districts of beautiful landscape known to me. The vast masses, the luxurious colouring, the mingled associations of great mountain scenery, amaze, excite, overwhelm, or exhaust – but too seldom teach; the mind cannot choose where to begin.

But Derbyshire is a lovely child's first alphabet; an alluring first lesson in all that is admirable; and powerful chiefly in the way it engages and fixes the attention. On its miniature cliffs a dark ivy leaf detaches itself as an object of importance; you distinguish with interest the species of mosses on the top; you count, like many falling diamonds, the magical drops of its petrifying wells; the cluster of violets in the shade is an Armida's garden to you – and the grace of it all! – and the suddenness of its enchanted changes, the terrorless grotesque – grotesque *par excellence*. It was a meadow a minute ago, now it is a cliff, and in an instant a cave – and here was a brooklet, and now it is a whisper underground. Turn but the corner of the path, and it is a little green lake of incredible crystal; and if the trout in it lifted up their heads and talked to you, you would be no more surprised than if it was in the Arabian Nights.

This is a famously bitter and much-quoted outburst from Ruskin's Fors Clavigera, *originally monthly 'Letters to the Workmen and Labourers of Great Britain', in 1896, about 'progress' in the infant arts of the telegraph and photography, and the construction of the Midland line (now the Monsal Trail) through the valley of the Wye.*

JOHN RUSKIN *Fors Clavigera: Letters to the Workmen and Labourers of Great Britain* (1896)

You think it a great triumph to make the sun draw brown landscapes for you. That was also a discovery, and some day may be useful. But the sun had drawn brown landscapes before for you, not in brown, but in green, and blue, and all imaginable colours, here in England. Not one of you ever looked at them then; not one of you cares for the loss of them now, when you have shut the sun out with smoke, so that he can draw nothing more, except brown blots through a hole in a box. There was a rocky valley between Bakewell and Buxton, once upon a time, divine as the Vale of Tempe; you might have seen the Gods there morning and evening – Apollo and all the sweet Muses of the light – walking in fair procession on the lawns of it, and to and fro among the pinnacles of its crags. You cared neither for Gods nor grass, but for cash (which you did not know the way to get); you thought you could get it by what *The Times* calls 'Railroad Enterprise'. You Enterprised a Railroad through the valley – you blasted its rocks away, heaped thousands of tons of shale into its lovely stream. They valley is gone, and the Gods with it; and now, every fool in Buxton can be at Bakewell in half an hour, and every fool in Bakewell at Buxton; which you think a lucrative process of exchange – you Fools Everywhere.

To talk at a distance, when you have nothing to say, though you were ever so near; to go fast from this place to that, with nothing to do at one end or the other: these are powers certainly. Much more, power of increased Production, if you, indeed, had got it, would be something to boast of. But are you so entirely sure that you *have* got it – that the mortal disease of plenty, and afflictive affluence of good things, are all you have to dread?

Not everyone shared Ruskin's outrage at the despoilation of the Wye valley by the Midland Railway. 'Strephon' was the pen name of Edward Bradbury, a Derby-born journalist who specialised in railway-related subjects, particularly the Midland Railway, for whom he worked for eighteen years.

Here Bradbury gives a Shakespearean spin to the other side of the argument. This is his vivid description of an exciting ride on the footplate of an engine on the former Midland line, part of which is now the Monsal Trail and part the Buxton–Manchester branch line, between Derby and Manchester.

There's also a delightful vignette of fictional passengers using the loop line at Miller's Dale, which linked it to the spa town of Buxton, and a florid description of the journey through the two-mile-long Dove Holes Tunnel, at the time the biggest engineering project the railway had undertaken.

EDWARD BRADBURY ('STREPHON') *All About Derbyshire* (1884)

The Midland Company justly claim for their route that it 'passes through the most picturesque portions of the Peak of Derbyshire and the Vale of Matlock'; but this description tremendously understates the charms of the ride. The windows of the 'bogie' carriage, or the Pullman car form an ever-changing panorama; but the scenery regarded from the footplate of the speeding engine is a railway romance. The courteous kindness of the Chief of the Locomotive Department of the Midland Railway provided me with a place on the engine of the Manchester express, and my only regret is that I had not John Ruskin for company, to have shown him sentiment in steam, romance in realism, fancy in fact, poetry in points and crossings, sermons in sleepers, songs in steel rails, books in signal-boxes, tongues in trenails, and good in all railway things.

Monsal Head Viaduct

Matlock Bath looks like an exquisite Swiss miniature, a Neufchatel in a nutshell. But we have not time for even a note of admiration. Another tunnel obliterates the pleasing prospect. The High Tor towers above us; a momentary glance at rock and river; and then the yawning darkness of yet another tunnel receives the train. Out again, and Matlock Bridge flies past with lightning-like velocity. Quick! And you will discern the aboriginal parish church, and Matlock Bank, with its temples sacred to hyydropathic horrors.

Now comes the isolated peak of Oker Hill; then Darley, with its tranquil old church, sheltered by a yew tree which was contemporaneous with Homer's heroes. What a maze of sidings there are at Rowsley; at Rowsley, the threshold of Haddon Hall and Chatsworth. Here the Wye and the Derwent fall into each other's arms; there is the 'Peacock', with its ivied mullioned windows, and quaint gables, and clustered chimneys and old-fashioned garden.

Presently we at the portals of the long tunnel which burrows under the time-hallowed towers of Haddon Hall. The Midland system was arrested at Rowsley for some time because His Grace the Duke of Rutland was opposed to the railway running in the valley past Haddon Hall, and so the line passes under the wooded hill-side upon which the feudal walls are reared. Perhaps it is best that it should be so. The baronial palace should be read slowly and studiously, like a book, room after room, from basement to battlements, not hurried past at the sensation pace of a mile a minute.

We are in the tunnel now with a swift procession of black goods trucks passing, which 'covered with palls, and gliding on like a weird funeral, convey themselves guiltily away, as if their freight had come to a secret and unlawful end'.

Out into the genial lights of day again, with the scent of meadow-sweet, instead of the smell of the damp mould. The Wye wanders in the fields in a hundred serpentine paths of its own choosing. There are views on either side – before, behind, to the right and to the left. The signal stands against us at Bakewell. The hiss of the 'Westinghouse' checks the speeding train. Tinkle! Tinkle! sounds the electric block-bell in the pointsman's box; down drops the horizontal arms of the tall semaphore; the steam is put on, and soon Bakewell, with its heaven-pointing spire, tucked in among the hills of the Peak, sinks behind. It is collar-work for the Iron Horse now. Up Hill, and no mistake.

Past Hassop and Longstone, with far-stretching darks moors climbing to the sky-line. Chay! chay! chay! again with distinct pants. The regulator is pushed on at the full. Curves and gradient. More coal, if you please. The locomotive, like the fat boy in the *Pickwick Papers*, is always demanding refreshment. The coal-laden shovel is scarcely ever absent from its hungry mouth, while its consumption of water shows a thirsty weakness for *aqua pura*, which ought to induce the Good Templars to make the Iron Horse their patron saint. But do not let us malign the active animal. A steam-pressure which runs up to 150 pounds to the square inch need some support, you know.

Monsal Dale carries us into a region of romantic enchantment. The Wye, winding under wooded bank and jutting cliff, is one of Nature's daintiest water-colour sketches. At Cressbrook the scenery reaches a climax of poetic beauty. But tunnel after tunnel robs us of its charms; and it is, moreover, tormenting to rush through this scenery and not be able to pause and enjoy it. One is inclined to bribe the engine-driver to 'pull up', and to superannuate the stoker and guards into silence . . . [it is] teasing . . . to rush through the panorama of the Peak and not be able to stop and drink in the scenic beauties at your leisure – to linger in the secluded glen where the greenery of the bank woos the glancing stream, to climb the stubborn hill and receive the guerdon with which nature rewards the arduous ascent.

The valley of the River Wye (1889)

A pause, if it please you, at Miller's Dale, where a little crowd of passengers await the train. Here Mr Salford, from Manchester, who has left his rheumatism and crutches behind at Buxton, gets nimbly in the express along with Mrs Salford, and the two Miss Salfords, one a charming symphony in silk, the other a dainty vignette in velvet. Mr Saltley, of Birmingham, very gouty and bound for Buxton, gets out, and there is an interchange of several other passengers. Now the guard blows his whistle to proceed again, and the engine answers with a scream. A stout gentleman, who carries a red nose and a fishing-rod, pants pathetically up the platform in a perspiration and a hurry. But he is just one puff too late, and in waiting for the next train he will have time to moralize on the evils of unpunctuality.

We are now running by the side of the Wye, on a terrace on the hill-side. The tunnel robs us of many charming pictures, but the ride is remarkable for sweet surprises in scenery. The train rushing from the mouth of one limestone tunnel, crosses the river bridge thrown high up above the wild beauty of Chee Dale, only to plunge into another vault. But that transitory flash of Chee Dale is one of the most remarkable 'bits' of the journey. The ravine along which we now thunder is Blackwell Mill Junction. That lonely cluster of houses is a row of isolated platelayers' cottages; that heap of ruined stone is Blackwell Mill; to the left is the loop line that runs round the rock side to Buxton.

Now we are climbing up the steep gradient along Great Rocks Dale. Peak Forest now, whose woods were once the refuge of wolves, and whose church – a sort of Gretna Green in the Peak – was the haven of runaway lovers. Soon Dove Holes is reached, and the line drops down towards Manchester through a tunnel two miles in length. The black obscurity now envelopes us – a detonating signal explodes with a loud report under the wheels, and the iron monster gives an unnatural scream, as though it had received a death-wound, and with palpitating heart and quivering sides pulls up in the Stygian vault. A caution signal sends us on at slackened speed, then a white light waved in the darkness puts the steam on again. That scream has sent strange echoes flying. Ten thousand and one noises seem to compete in a clattering chorus of deafening, deadening din. The darkness may be felt. Sulphur fumes are added to the damp earthly smell. The circle of white light, thrown out by the furnace-fire, makes ghastly the faces of the enginemen at their post, peering through the gloom. A reverberating rumble is heard quite near. Two red ogre-eyes are burning their way through the darkness. In another second an avalanche of thunder and lightning is hurled past on the 'up-line' with awful velocity. With a shriek, and a rattle, and a roar, on and still on. Fantastic flakes of fire flutter from the engine chimney, and fly fitfully overhead. Now and again an air-shaft in the tunnel-roof sends down a delusive glimmer of day. Right in front is the tunnel-mouth, in size looking like a threepenny bit: it gets larger: now it assumes the dimensions of a sixpence: it grows into a shilling: soon it appears like a florin, and presently resembles a five shilling piece. Another half-minute in this vile vault, and then we burst into summer sunshine again. Viaducts carry us over Chapel-en-le-Frith, and give us Admodeus-like privileges with regard to peeping down cottage chimneys and into bed-room windows.

Down the hill-side now as if the Iron Horse were a frightened Pegasus and were running away altogether. The steam is shut off; ever and anon the sibilant sound of the air brake is heard. That station I think was New Mills; but the pace is so rapid that the letters on the platform name-board were running into each other. The rivulet running by the line is the Kinderbrook. To the right, Kinderscout – the king of the Peak mountains – sets his shoulders against the sky.

This is Bradbury's description of The Roaches and Lud's Church, in the Staffordshire Moorlands, from his earlier book, In the Derbyshire Highlands*:*

EDWARD BRADBURY ('STREPHON') *In the Derbyshire Highlands: Highways, Byeways and My Ways in the Peake Countrie* (1881)

ROUND BY THE ROCHES, WITH A LOOK AT LUDCHURCH

The dark, weather-worn Castle Rocks stand out from the wooded hill, and impend their pinnacles over a curve of deep valley at the bottom of which the Dane shines amid a dense green lining of spruce and larch. Beyond the gleam of water and the gloom of wood in the valley, the hills spread for miles, wild tracts of bronzed heath under the wide sphere of uninterrupted sky, here and there broken by a bright patch of emerald pasture, washed a cleaner green by recent rains, with white farmsteads standing out against the blue-black pines, such as Turner loved to introduce in the shading of his pictures. Some of these isolated buildings are sheltered in the dip of moorland valleys; others are perched like eyries on the brow of hills tight against the distant sky-line, with the sun flashing heliostate signals from their narrow window panes. All around is the fascination of great breadths of undulating spaces, and the spell of sunlight silence. To-morrow the whole sharp clear pictures may be sponged out by the grey soaking mists that brood over these hills and blot out every outline.

[Another walker] is asking . . .the bearings of Ludchurch, which he cannot find. No wonder he has missed it. Ninety-nine explorers out of a hundred would miss it. Ludchurch is close by. A narrow cleft in the wooded hill-side is the doorway. It leads to a flight of rough-hewn steps of slippery stone. We descend.

The riven rock, fern-covered and lichen-stained, rises on either side of us in a sheer precipice. The Church is really a gorge in the gritstone, some 200 yards in length, several yards in width, some 40 feet in depth, and with a narrow entrance at either end. Young ash-trees and hazels form a roof of luminous green, rare plants and ferns and dwarf trees spring from every cleft; cool mosses robe the naked rocks; high up in a

Doxey Pool on The Roaches

hazardous interstice a hawk has built its nest. At the further end of the Church a narrow slanting fissure opens out into an inner cavern ending in a perpendicular abyss which the most daring have not penetrated.

Luckily the guide-book writers are ignorant of Ludchurch, and excursionists are unable to find it. For the sacred temple would be violated by the fern-gatherers and botanists, who ruthlessly tear out the leaves from the great, green, God-written Book of Nature, and who kidnap sweet ferns and flowers, lichens and mosses, and carry them away into captivity to pine away, pale prisoners, far from the nourishing influences, the dews and wind and shade and sweet air of their native hills.

There is something ineffably solemn about this romantic ravine. A lovable little friend of mine once asked when she was here during a passing thunderstorm: 'Father, is this the place where God makes the thunder?' Sterner minds might almost endorse her tender fancy. This divine defile is linked with legend and history. Here Robin Hood, and

Lud's Church, with the face of the Green Knight

his gigantic Little John, and his Sherwood out-laws, met to receive the benediction of their 'curtal Friar'.

The persecuted Lollards, hunted down by the blood-hounds of persecution, sought refuge in Ludchurch, consecrating it by prayer and praise, sermon and psalm, and even baptising the walls with their blood . . . Walter De Lud-auk, the grey-haired Apostle of the proscribed Wickliffites, leading the simple devotions of his fervent followers. Close by him, his grand-daughter Alice, with her sylph-like figure, her streaming hair, her sweet face, her dulcet voice. She stands like May at the side of December, a picture of opening summer and declining winter. The fierce soldiers of Henry V bursting, without warning, upon the sequestered worshippers. The beautiful Alice lying killed in the assault by a shot from an arquebus, just when her escape is being made good by one of the Lollards, her lover, one Henrick Montair, a sturdy forester, equipped with crossbow and broad sword.

Or an historical painter might find a picturesque subject in a more modern grouping of which Ludchurch was the scene, when the Pretender and his Highlanders camped in the ravine on their ill-starred march to Derby in the winter of '45, with Flora Macdonald, whose ringlets steal from under a slouching military hat, as she nurses her heroic hopes on the very spot where the December winds wails a requiem over the dust of Alice De Lad-Auk.

Ludchurch at its extreme end leads up an ascent of rugged steps out on to the open moor. We are above Back Forest now. The entrance to its sylvan chapel is like a mouse-hole in a wall of green. Wide is the horizon from this wind-swept height. On one side the moors of Derbyshire and Cheshire stretch in bleak hungry solitudes with intersecting walls of grey-stone; while lo! on the other side reposes a vision of smiling farmsteads, and level meadows and green hedgerows. And that sunny dream is Staffordshire. It is a striking scenic contrast. In front, a wild Scotch picture, up in the land of Lorne somewhere, behind a fair gentle English landscape.

And so we tramp on through bog and bracken and bilberry, and the ever present purple heather bloom, 1,600 feet above the sea. The plover decoys us from its nest; ever and anon grouse rise strong on the wing in front. Three miles in length, the Roches are some two miles in breadth. The course lies from end to end of the rugged ridge, and our progress is inspired by 'the live translucent bath of air', as vitalising as the elusive Elixir of Life, which has been the search of the ages. Very bold and romantic is the scenery, almost unknown to painters. A quaint shrewd book published a century and a half ago (Dr Robert Plot's *History of Staffordshire*), says:

> Here are vast rocks which surprise with admiration, called the Henclouds and the Leek Roaches. They are of so great a height, and afford such stupendous prospects, that one could hardly believe that they were anywhere to be found but in picture. They are so bare that they have no turf upon them, nor indeed any earth to produce it; which whether they were so from the Creation, or were uncovered by the general Flood, or were washed clean by rain, it is not possible to account for.

Our walk along the ridge is a romance in rock. Black, sepulchral, and uncanny rise the rugged millstone-grit crags above the broad undulations of heather. They assume strange shapes. Now a massive block, tapering at the end, and poised over a plateau, suggests a great breech-loader pointed at some far-off threatening mountain fort. Another stands an inscrutable eternal Presence, a sphinx indifferent to time, and unchanged by Age, a melancholy Menhir, silent, awful, with the secret of a pre-historic crisis hidden beneath its scarred, storm-rent breast. Other rocks, like colossal dragons, and petrified lions; and still others, weather worn and wrinkled, which remind one of the monsters of antediluvian birth, with grotesque heads, turned-up noses, blinking eyes, and mouths leering horridly. Here is a rocking stone; there is a large-sized dolmen. And then, behold! at the summit of this ridge, close by where the sappers and miners have raised their flagstaff cairn, is a lonely, rush-fringed tarn, called Doxey Pool, whose peat-coloured water catches the sunlight like a shield of steel.

Still we have the awful cataclysm of crags around us, scattered like the brooding monuments of a dead world, the Necropolis of fabled giants. One upright on a higher ridge; the other prostate on a lower plateau that shelves abruptly into the valley. On the crags are shoals of fossil fish; underneath, seams of coal and ironstone. I merely mention the fact as a curiosity. For neither of us regard the country with the mercenary manufacturing eye of the Philistines to whom the map of England is a geological chart representing coal measures and iron ore, and who look upon Cornwall as a tin mine, and North Wales as a big slate quarry, and the white crags of Derbyshire as containing so many cubic yards of pure limestone.

A little further on and a bridle-path, breast-high in bracken, leads us to Rock Hall, where there is another dolmen sculptured by the axe of God. Be not deceived by the appellation 'hall'. It is not the synonym in this instance for an ample country-seat and architectural stateliness. Rock Hall is simply a bleak keeper's lodge beneath the beetling cliffs. It belongs to Squire Brocklehurst, the owner of the Swythamley estate. There are antlers over the door, and black old oak within. Part of the retreat is a natural cave made cosy with furniture that shines like a smile. Another room is stone-built.

We are welcomed to Rock Hall by a country-woman with broad dialect and apple-like face, streaked with red, like a Normandy pippin. She wears a tall snowy cap that makes her resemble a Breton peasant. Did she often see visitors? Oh yes, she had received Royalty, for had not the Prince and Princess Teck taken tea with her when their Highnesses were shooting in this neighbourhood? This comforting fact compensates the old lady for years of solitude. We have milk and sweet brown-bread and butter here, which is as acceptable to our freshened appetite as the most toothsome dishes ever packed in one of Fortnum and Mason's hampers.

The following excerpt is from a little-known short story by Arthur Conan Doyle (1859–1930), the Scottish physician and author, most famously the creator of the master sleuth, Sherlock Holmes.

ARTHUR CONAN DOYLE *The Terror of Blue John Gap* (1910)

It is a most lonely spot, and the walks are picturesque in the extreme. The farm consists of grazing land lying at the bottom of an irregular valley. On each side are the fantastic limestone hills, formed of rock so soft that you can break it away with your hands. All this country is hollow. Could you strike it with with some gigantic hammer it would boom like a drum, or possibly cave in altogether and expose some huge subterranean sea. A great sea there must surely be, for on all sides the streams run into the mountain itself, never to reappear. There are gaps everywhere amid the rocks, and when you pass through them you find yourself in great caverns, which wind down into the bowels of the earth. I have a small bicycle lamp, and it is a perpetual joy to me to carry it into these weird solitudes, and see the wonderful silver and black effects when I throw its light upon the stalactites which drape the lofty roofs. Shut off the lamp, and you are in the blackest darkness. Turn it on, and it is a scene from the Arabian Nights.

4.
THE LOCAL INFLUENCE

Although the Peak may not have been blessed with many visits from the great painters, it has produced some fine writers on its own account. 'Peakrills' (the old name for Peak dwellers) like the pioneer archaeologist Thomas Bateman, Crichton Porteous, S.P.B. Mais and Ethel Gallimore waxed lyrical about the hills and dales of their beloved homeland.

Thomas Bateman of Lomerdale Hall, Middleton-by-Youlgrave, sometimes known as the Barrow Knight, was a pioneering Victorian antiquarian and archaeologist who was also a prodigious barrow-digger. It has been estimated that he and his associates dug into nearly 400 tumuli in his short lifetime (he died in 1861 at the age of thirty-nine), and in 1845 alone he delved into no fewer than thirty-eight Peak District tumuli. Evidence of his excavations can still be seen in the craters which mark most of their tops.

Although modern archaeologists are sometimes scornful at Bateman's unscientific methods, he at least recorded what he found. He published his results in two books, Vestiges of the Antiquities of Derbyshire *(1848), and in* Ten Years' Diggings in Celtic and Saxon Grave Hills, *published just days before his death in 1861.*

The following two excerpts record Bateman's evocative description of the Peak's most famous prehistoric monument of Arbor Low, near Monyash, from Vestiges, *and the disastrous excavation of the nearby Neolithic burial mound of Gib Hill in 1848 from* Ten Years' Diggings.

Having failed to find anything much in trenches driven from the top, a tunnel dug into the western side of the mound suddenly collapsed, smashing a 'very pretty' funereal urn under the weight of the falling stone cist (stone-lined grave) from above. The massive limestone cist was removed and re-erected in Bateman's garden at Lomberdale Hall, but has since been returned to its place of origin.

THOMAS BATEMAN *Vestiges of the Antiquities of Derbyshire* (1848)

By far the most important, as well as the most uninjured, remain of the religious edifices of our barbarous forefathers that is to be found in the midland counties, is to be seen a short distance to the left hand of the turnpike road from Buxton to Ashbourne, at about an equal distance from each of those towns. This is the famous temple of Arbor Lowe, or Arbe Lowe, as it is generally called by the country people; it is a circle of large unhewn limestones, surrounded by a deep ditch, outside of which rises a large and high vallum. Its situation, though considerably elevated, is not so high as some eminences in the neighbouring country; yet it commands an extensive view, especially towards the north-east, in which direction the dreary and sombre wastes of the heath-clad East Moor are perfectly visible, though distant about fifteen miles; were it not for a few stone fences, which intervene in the foreground, the solitude of the place and the boundless view of an uncultivated country are such as almost carry the observer back through a multitude of centuries, and make him believe that he sees the same view and the same state of things as existed in the days of the architects of this once holy fane.

The feelings on visiting this place, on a warm summer's day, when there is no sound to disturb the solitude, save the singing of the lark, and now and then the cry of the plover (both which here abound), are truly delightful. But to resume the description; the area encompassed by the ditch is about fifty yards in diameter, and of a circular form; though, from a little declination of the ground towards the north, it appears somewhat elliptical when viewed from particular points. The stones which compose the circle are rough, unhewn masses of limestone, apparently thirty in number; but this cannot be determined with certainty, as several of them are broken; most of them are from six to eight feet in length, and three or four broad in the widest part; their thickness is more variable, and their respective shapes are different and indescribable. They all lie upon the ground, many in an oblique position, but the opinion that has prevailed, of the narrowest end of each being pointed towards the centre, in order to represent the rays of the sun, and prove that luminary to

Arbor Low, by Nelly Erichsen (1905)

Arbor Low, by Karen Frenkel (2012)

have been the object of worship, must have arisen from inaccurate observation, for they almost as frequently point towards the ditch as otherwise; whether they ever stood upright, as most of the stones of druidical circles do, is an inquiry not easy to determine; though Mr Pilkington was informed that a very old man, living in Middleton, remembered, when a boy, to have seen them standing obliquely on one end; this secondary kind of evidence does not seem entitled to much credit, as the soil at the basis of the stones does not appear to have ever been removed to a depth sufficient to ensure the possibility of the stones being placed in an erect position. Within the circle are some smaller stones scattered irregularly, and near the centre are three larger ones, by some supposed to have formed a cromlech or altar, but there are no perceptible grounds for such an opinion. The width of the ditch, which immediately surrounds the area on which the stones are placed, is about six yards; the height of the bank or vallum, on the inside (though much reduced by the unsparing hand of time), is still from six to eight yards; but this varies throughout the whole circumference, which, on the top, is about two hundred and seventy yards. The vallum is chiefly formed of the earth thrown out of the ditch, besides which a little has been added from the ground which immediately surrounds the exterior of the vallum, thus adding to its height, and to the imposing appearance it presents to any one approaching from a distance. To the inclosed area are two entrances, each of the width of ten or twelve yards, and opening towards the north and south. On the east side of the southern entrance is a large barrow, standing in the same line of circumference as the vallum, but wholly detached except at the base. This barrow has been several times unsuccessfully examined, and remained an antiquarian problem until the summer of the year 1845, when the original interment was discovered, of a nature to prove beyond doubt the extreme antiquity of the tumulus, and consequently of the temple. About a quarter of a mile from Arbor Lowe, in a westerly direction, is a large conical tumulus, known as Gib Hill, which is connected with the vallum of the temple, by a rampire of earth, running in a serpentine direction, not dissimilar to the avenue through the celebrated temple of Abury; to any believer in the serpent worship of the Celtic tribes this fact will be of interest.

THOMAS BATEMAN *Ten Years' Diggings in Celtic and Saxon Grave Hills* (1861)

The large barrow upon Middleton Moor, called Gib Hill, situated about 350 yards west from the circular temple of Arborlow, and connected with it by a serpentine ridge of earth, had been previously examined by the late Mr. William Bateman, in 1824, without much success. From the analogy borne by Arborlow and its satellite, Gib Hill, to the plan of Abury with its avenue of stones terminating in a lesser circle on the Hak Pen range of hills, no less than by the remarkable similarity of the names, I had ever reckoned this tumulus to be of more than common importance, under the supposition that a successful excavation of it might yield some approximate data respecting the obscure period of the foundation of the neighbouring circle.

Owing to the large size of the mound, our operations extended over several days, the result of each being noticed diary-wise as at once the most simple and intelligible arrangement.

January 10th was occupied in removing the upper part of the hill, the trench being commenced about half-way up its side, pretty much in the line of the former opening. A few splinters of animal bone and a flake of calcined flint, only, were the product of the day.

January 11th – The cutting was carried forwards to the intended limit beyond the centre of the barrow, yielding in its progress more animal bones, a dog's tooth, numerous calcined flakes of flint, and a neatly formed arrow head of the same substance.

January 12th – The trench being widened at each side, a space nearly, but not exactly, in the centre of the barrow, was found to consist of loose stones, whilst the outer part of the mound exposed to view by the section, was composed of tempered earth approaching the consistence of hard clay. In the course of this day a small piece of the border of an ornamented urn, a circular instrument, an arrow point, and many chippings of flint were found.

January 13th was passed in deepening the trench, principally through the before-named clay, varied by layers of decomposed wood and charcoal. From the appearance of the bark still remaining on some of these fragments, they were decided to be hazel. Amongst them were found animal bones and flints as before, one of the latter being a fine instrument of semicircular shape.

January 14th – Our excavation was continued until the undisturbed surface of the earth was reached and laid bare for the space of 25 feet by 18, without disclosing any interment whatever; the appearance presented by the section of the barrow, here about 15 feet high, thus making it evident that the tumulus had been originally raised over four smaller mounds, each consisting of indurated clay intermixed with wood and charcoal, the superimposed materials being of a looser description. On the natural soil beneath the little mounds were flints as usual, one of them a round instrument, and large disconnected bones of oxen very much decayed.

January 15th – A tunnel was driven from the west side of the trench at right angles, in the hope of finding an interment, but after carrying it three or four yards it was deemed unsafe to continue it; and the supporting timbers being knocked away previous to abandoning the work, the whole superstructure fell in, and, much to our surprise, revealed the interment near the top of the mound, which we had been so laboriously seeking at its base. This consisted of a rectangular cist, measuring inside 2 feet 6 inches by 2 feet, composed of four massive blocks of limestone, covered in by a fifth of irregular form, averaging 4 feet square by 10 inches thick. The cap-stone was not more than eighteen inches beneath the turf clothing the summit of the barrow; in fact the men had been working directly under the cist for some time. By the sudden fall of two of the sides and the adjacent earth, a very pretty vase of small size was crushed to pieces, the fragments mingling with the burnt human bones in company with which it had for ages occupied the sepulchral chamber. The urn measuring 41 inches in height, has since been restored almost to its original perfection; it is of that class of vessels indifferently deposited with human remains, burnt or unburnt, and which may probably have contained food or drink, but never the remains, as is the case with cinerary urns. A review of these facts leads to the conclusion that Gib Hill was not in the first instance a sepulchral mound, so large a portion of the interior having been removed down to the natural rock without any deposit of human remains being found, it appears impossible for any interment to have escaped observation at the base of the tumulus, where it would naturally have been placed at the time of its formation, had any such existed.

January 17th – A molar tooth from the lower jaw of a horse, and a piece of white flint, were found in the rubbish that had fallen out of the cist the day before. The cist itself was removed and re-erected in conformity with its original plan, in the garden at Lomberdale House, where it now remains.

Although Crichton Porteous (1901–91) was not born in Derbyshire, he spent most of his childhood holidays with his uncle at Bugsworth (now Buxworth). He was a true countryman and the prolific author of a number of books on what he later regarded as his home county. Coming from farming stock, he was particularly good on rural affairs and this is reflected in his writing. Porteous defended the charms of Derbyshire with a Peakrill's zeal, as is shown in this excerpt from his 1954 book Peakland, *and in the section on Mam Tor from his* Derbyshire *(1950).*

CRICHTON PORTEOUS *Peakland* (1954)

A Peakrill, returned from many years in British Columbia, when asked which was the most beautiful country he had seen, replied unhesitatingly:

'This right here.'

'But the prairies?'

'Wonderful,' he said. 'Everything you've ever heard or read is true. When you first see them – the farmlands extending out of sight – it seems the most marvellous country there can be. But after twenty-four hours of apparently endless sameness it begins to pall. You reach the Rockies. Ah, again everything's wonderful. Bouldered streams with white water, peaks and pine forest nothing could be better, But after several hundred miles all alike, satiety. A man wants variety, and here you have it.'

But, being a Peakrill, obviously he was biased!

Shortly before the war ended I began a tour of every county in England and Wales. Approximately half the tour had been made when an acquaintance asked which area I liked best.

'Peakland.'

He smiled. 'Yes, I know you live there, and in a beautiful part, but seriously, out of all you've seen, which do you consider the best?'

I hesitated, then gave the same reply.

'But you don't honestly mean that,' he retorted with some acerbity, 'you can't do. Have you been to Kent yet?'

'No.'

'Ah!' he said, his good temper instantly restored.

So I anticipated Kent pleasurably, and was lucky. It was cherry time, and I was taken through the best orchards. Twenty, even thirty, acres in extent some of them, all the trees in precise lines – crosswise, diagonalwise – mostly bush-trees, so that the fruit was all within reach, scarcely a ladder needed. And there the cherries hung, white, scarlet, crimson, maroon, lit by a brilliant sun like thousands of tiny Chinese lanterns shining above smooth-mown turf. I was taken to sheds where hundreds of stacked baskets waited for market, and was offered my choice, as many baskets as I wanted, free. Indeed, I came away with coloured memories of Kent! It really was a most delightful county; and I continued to think for quite a time that perhaps it was the best.

I thought that way till one day motoring south from Derby into Leicestershire we stopped to eat sandwiches on the roadside grass. We were still in Derbyshire, and all at once it came to me how the country displayed eastwards was like certain lovely parts of Kent. Similar gentle undulations bore partly hidden farms, and there were orchards – not

View into Hope Dale from the Winnats Pass, Castleton (1889)

cherry orchards, admitted, but orchards rich with sunning apples and mellowing pears. The only picturesque detail lacking was the white-cowled oast-houses, but oast-houses are not enough to give any county priority above another. So I began to ask seriously whether Kent, after all, should be put so high.

I recalled the clean, upward-flowing sweeps of the North Downs, but were there not similar smoothly rounded and impressive heights by Ashburne running north to Buxton? And I asked, where were the dales in Kent to compare with those of Dove and Lathkill?

Then I began to consider other counties.

Westmorland's mountains and lakes – but had not Kinder Scout in certain moods a somewhat similar sombre majesty, and were not some Peakland lakes (artificial, indeed, yet very natural seeming) worth talking of? I pictured great curved faces of Northumberland fells leaning from the North Sea to form England's backbone, and for comparison marshalled Thorpe Cloud, High Wheeldon and Axe Edge, much lower, yet conveying to a tolerant onlooker very similar impressions of supine strength and vast space.

Nearly every striking feature of every other county, I eventually realised, was represented, and quite admirably represented, excepting only certain coastal beauties. But no fewer than eighteen English and eight Welsh counties shout of their maritime scenery, so that it is obviously too common a possession to be envied. And is not much coast scenery overrated? The level but attractive and mysterious sea often gives an illusory height and dignity to cliffs that are truly neither very tall nor very dignified. The so-called white cliffs of Dover owe a lot to sentiment. And I remember motoring to Devon to view 'red cliffs' there, and only realising on the return, passing the Roaches, that Peakland has its own cliffs that make a journey of several hundreds of miles to see those of the West Country a needless whim.

Therefore, after all, my opinion was strengthened that Derbyshire is the best county, a sort of jewel enclosed in the rest of England as in a casket; and though thus far I have written Derbyshire, it was only to be able to refer to that warm pastoral part south of the county town as rivalling Kent; otherwise I could have written Peakland throughout, for in Peakland is contained the very best of Derbyshire.

But, although not born in Peakland, maybe I, too, am biased!

A motorist coasting down a valley saw a walker with a bulky pack, and hesitated. An unsolicited offer of a lift is not always welcomed. This young man, however, bowed politely – a Swiss, he said.

'These trifling hills!' exclaimed the motorist. 'What is there here to make it worth your time?'

'Your hills are small, yes,' said the Swiss, 'but round my home everything is brilliant and hard – blue skies like glass, red flowers, purple flowers, black rocks, snow to blind you – here, everything softened by haze and shadows into half-tones. That is what I come for,' and he indicated a mist like a glaze on the near hillside, 'nothing to equal that in Switzerland'.

A relative from South Africa came to stay near Chapel-en-leFrith. One afternoon we walked towards White Hall and climbed nearly to the top of Combs Valley, where arriving at a gateway we turned to look through, across at the Moss.

'My word, that's exactly South Africa – at its best!' he exclaimed, as it seemed involuntarily.

'At its best?'

'After the rains, when everything's fresh. It keeps beautiful like this for a few weeks, then all goes brown.'

Actually just then there was drought in many English counties, for it was the end of summer. The central plain around Bedford was burnt up. But with us valleys and hills were almost as in April. Peakland is prolific of mists and drifting rains, and these, together with many running springs, give it the special glory of its ever green turf as well as providing the softened, changing colours and shadows that the Swiss visitor praised.

Fascinating it is to note the same hills day by day. Sometimes they look subdued and small, and then may appear to increase in stature and stalwartness till they seem to challenge Alpine heights. The illusion can be helped by clouds that settle on the long flat summits and often conform with such peculiar faithfulness that it is impossible to tell where hill ceases and cloud begins. Some dawns show the hills plum-blue and ethereal as if fashioned of wood-smoke; at dusk there may be a shy blush-rose beauty; in later dusk the hills may stand stark and perpendicular like fences of grey steel. And one morning I saw the hills like gleaming bubbles of pure glass. Much snow had lain for several days, then there had been a brief night thaw followed by an intense dawn freeze with a white sun, and the hills had been encased in the most fragile crystal.

Well, a region with such beauty – that can challenge the rest of England, Canada, South Africa and Switzerland – is worth writing about!

CRICHTON PORTEOUS *Derbyshire* (1950)

So we come to what I believe is the deepest secret of Derbyshire's inspiration. Not only do conditions draw out fine qualities of men now: through the ages these conditions have operated. Here men continually have fought and won or failed, and the evidence of this fighting remains more prolifically than anywhere else that I know.

Where is there a county with more remains of those pre-Roman peoples about whom so little is known? And these remains are not railed off; very few are protected except by being on private land, land over which few persons would hesitate to trespass, because there are no crops to spoil, there being no depth of earth. Which explains also why these remains have never been ploughed up. Land has always been plentiful. If something was in one spot, why trouble to remove it? Try some other spot. And so these evidences of the past remain to tell of the unknown men who lived and struggled and then died. Everywhere one feels linked with the past. One sees the end of so much dreaming, planning, working, one cannot but feel humble; and then, above all, comes pride that men should have striven so, and should still strive, and one feels that one's place is in the strife too. What if all does come to nought, it is fine to have fought, to have left a trace, even though at the last it may seem to be so little. That is the feeling that I get.

How good it is to go up steep Mam Tor (Mother Hill?) by the sheep track, with the hard wind coming up from the dark mist on a day when that is all, with the vague darker bulks of the encompassing hills, that is to be seen of Castleton and Hope Valley. Here are the great earthworks, concentric rings, how many hundreds of years old? Still there; save where the Tor is slowly sliding to destruction, victim of weathering.

What manner of people built these earthworks? Hardy they must have been, for nowhere in Derbyshire does the wind drive more roughly or snow hiss more viciously. They were not a skulking people but a proud, for there is defiance in the set of the lines they built; and the height and length of the lines show that they were not puny-minded. I have had here the same feeling as the first time at the Forth Bridge: that I was looking at an undertaking only possible to men of courage and forward-looking minds, and I felt humble before it.

From the top of Mam Tor on clearer days one gets the finest view of the new road that has been made at such great cost of money, time, and effort, round the foot of the shale slide that has given the tor the name 'Shivering Mountain'. There the road is, snake-like, almost doubled on itself, another piece of man's enterprise; and from Mam Tor top can be seen also the last reach of that other road of the Winniates [*sic*]. Coming up between the lofty towers and walls of limestone which throw always a slight shadow there, one's thoughts swing inevitably to the earlier men who chose this as the most obvious way, though very steep, to Mam Tor fort and the long shallow plateau of Rushup. Close by the pass is Odin Mine, worked we know not how long, and that other cavern of the strange blue-veined rock that the Romans are believed to have prized but knew not as Blue John. All this is land of history, not the history of births and deaths of kings and of the notorious, but the history of ordinary

Lion's Head Dovedale

folk who were the private soldiers, the road builders, and the miners of other days. It is impossible not to feel the linking up of present life with the past here.

Except for the new road only evidences of the men of the times that we think of as very far past have yet been mentioned, and it is natural that there should be many more signs of men of closer times. Take the quarries hollowed out of so many hills. Quarries in such unexpected places that we are puzzled for what purpose stone could have been wanted there. Yet men dug and hewed with some purpose, were eager, hopeful, got, we suppose, what they wanted, and then left and slowly the turf crept over the scarred rock and took it under its easeful cloak once more.

Along this Rushup plateau men are quarrying again. Near Eldon Hole, which the men who garrisoned Mam Tor no doubt knew, the side of the hill is being cut away in great benches by pneumatic drills. The crushing plant trembles the corrugated iron tower in which it is housed, and seems a monstrous thing, dominating with its roar a surrounding half-mile of country. Only here industry is in true perspective, for the men working on the benches look midgets against the long swelling outline of the higher hill; the sound of the shots that burst and hurl sharp rock fragments over the squat buildings that are like air-raid shelters is lost in the wide sky almost as easily as a cuckoo call. In our cities industry impresses as it never can do here, and climbing the nearly obliterated track by the present workings on to the top of Eldon Hill and finding the turfed-over holes and gashes made by earlier men, one realises that in due course time will win over what is now being done. And yet there is something exhilarating in seeing man's effort going on, continuing that endless story of effort that has been put forth so often, and has paused and started again, and paused and restarted till now.

A mile across Eldon Hill and the roar and popping of the quarry becomes only memory, and here is a round pond holding dark still water, which the breeze roughens a little at the eastern end as though it were sleek black fur being rubbed the wrong way by an invisible hand. Some man thought and planned, and then carted and put in carefully the stones with which the shallow hollow is lined. And here his handiwork lies with not even a sheep near, yet is the pond another gage thrown down, as it were, against nature in the fight that began with life and must go on till life ends. There is something fine, I repeat, in these evidences that lie everywhere of man's never-ending battling, which has always, so far as we may judge, been but a forlorn hope though never undertaken as a forlorn hope; always man fighting with the ideal of ultimate victory.

S.P.B. (Petre) Mais (1885–1975), dubbed 'the Ambassador of the Countryside', was during the 1930s and 1940s, one of the best-known broadcasters and authors in Britain.

Mais came to live at The Rectory, Tansley, near Matlock, in 1889 at the age of four when his father was appointed rector there, and the hills and dales of Derbyshire awoke in him an unquenchable love and lifelong interest in the countryside. He later wrote that his childhood and impressionable years were spent in Derbyshire, and it was the county that he invariably thought of when he thought of home.

He was the author of over 200 books on the British countryside, and the man who presented a 'Letter from America' for BBC Radio thirteen years before Alistair Cooke. He also wrote about poverty and unemployment in the northern counties long before J.B. Priestley and George Orwell, and was a tireless benefactor of the jobless and homeless during the Great Depression of the 1930s.

S.P.B. MAIS *The Highlands of Britain* (1932)

THE PEAK

Derbyshire is known to and loved by the Lancastrian and Yorkist, both of whom are men of impeccable taste in scenery; but it is much less well known than it ought to be among Southerners, who have a vague idea that Buxton exists only for the winter sportsman, and that the whole country is grey and forbidding. The truth is that, for natural beauty, it ranks among the very highest. I think the Lakes eclipse it, but its only other competitors (in England) are Yorkshire, Devon, and Cornwall, which have the advantage, if it is an advantage, of the sea. Certainly no other county has such variety.

Each Sunday morning the railway-station platforms of Manchester are crowded with walkers bent on conquering the high plateaus of Kinder Scout or Bleaklow.

The Peak, which has no peak, is unfortunately mainly preserved as a grouse moor, but, after years of fighting, certain privileges in the way of foot-paths have been conceded to the general public.

Cave Dale

I don't very much care for keeping to a path on an open moor, and I don't think that the health of a grouse is quite so important as the health of the city-worker, but I don't supposed that men who are rich enough to own grouse moors have much sympathy with the man who merely wants a free open space to walk over. The only solution is for the nation to acquire these moors, and banish the grouse to an area where they are less likely to be disturbed.

Certainly the Kinder Scout plateau is about as wild a bit of moorland as we have in England. Its edge is marked by a vertical slab of rock under the summit, and on the summit there rise a few craggy odd-shaped tors. There are many treacherous patches of bog on all these moors, and it is extremely easy to lose one's way in the mist. In view of its comparatively small area, it is strange how many people have lost their lives up here. The height is only 2,000 feet, and the area covered by it negligible when we compare it with the Highlands. But is has the power to awe us if we stray in bad weather, and it is no place to climb without map and compass. I usually make my ascent from Glossop, which provides an extra walk by way of the Doctor's Gate, and, at the Snake Inn, a lonely house over the brow of the Sheffield road, I turn up Ashop Clough, which runs parallel with the edge. The only quarrel I have with this is the presence of too many grouse, who stand about and harshly rattle their machine-gun-like throats, and the presence of too many notice-boards along the almost too well-defined track.

S.P.B. MAIS *This Unknown Island* (1933)

Now Derbyshire *is* an unknown country. And this I find very odd, for, as Ruskin discovered, it is a lovely child's alphabet, an alluring first lesson in all that is admirable.

It is a sort of Lilliput England, enshrined in the very heart of England, with all England's most characteristic beauties reproduced in miniature – her wild moors, her cliffs, her winding rivers, her woods and her meadows, her medieval manor houses, superb churches and compact, dignified villages.

If all England were lost but this one small midland county, you could still in after years rebuild the old England from this perfect model of her, for she is not only *in* the heart of England, she *is* the heart of England.

Other counties have undergone a sea-change. Prosperity has smiled on them and they have become, in the words of uncompromising Derbyshire, 'soft'. Derbyshire has not gone soft, nor ever will. She is an unchanging as the Sphinx. The same families that were of good report here in the Middle Ages are still here, and still of good report.

They do not plough the soft, yielding earth. They blast it with dynamite to quarry the stone. They sunk shafts to the very bowels of the earth to follow the seams of coal. They wander along subterranean caverns that were old when the Romans found them, in search of lead.

If you have hitherto avoided Derbyshire it cannot be because of the people, because in them you will recognize yourself at your best and most

English, unspoiled by any veneer of affectation. That their candour is to some natures disconcerting and misleading is apparent in Mr Hilaire Belloc's poem describing the Midlands as sodden and unkind. He could not have hit upon two words less applicable.

Whatever else has kept you from Derbyshire it can't be the scenery. Bryon meant it when he said that Derbyshire possesses scenery as *noble* as any in Greece or Switzerland. *Noble* is the word. Sublimity does not depend on size but symmetry. Dovedale is just as satisfying as the Jungfrau.

Ethel Gallimore was a leading figure in the protection of her beloved Peak District for well over half a century. The daughter of Sheffield industrialist T.W. Ward, she was the founding secretary of the Sheffield Association for the Protection of Local Scenery in 1924, which later became the Sheffield branch of the Council for the Protection of Rural England (now the Campaign to Protect Rural England and Friends of the Peak District).

She later married the assistant secretary, architect and planner Gerald Haythornthwaite, and they worked tirelessly together in the protection of their beloved Peak District for fifty years. Gerald was in fact responsible for drawing up the boundaries of the Peak District National Park, and became a forceful and influential chairman of its Planning Control Committee for many years.

ETHEL BASSETT GALLIMORE *The Pride of the Peak* (1926)

Froggatt Edge, Curbar Edge, and Baslow Edge
I will go up, I will go all alone

Curbar Edge

Up to the moors, the blue and cloudy sky;
Even to those fierce rands (edges) of blackened stone
Whose ramparts sharp across the moorlands lie:
Where lies the water black and cold,
Where gleams the bracken tipped with gold,
Beside the grasses pale and by the sedge,
On high above the cliffs of Froggatt Edge.

Boldly the boulders o'er the valley stand,
And lift their heads against the lofty air;
Their jutting crags command the lower land,
Like couchant dragons looking from their lair.
And near a chasm, high and deep,
Enwalled with whinstone, swart and steep,

A tortuous stump, maniacally glad
Twists high above the rout of rochers [rocks] mad.

And where the way is mossy and most fair,
And most the heath grows by the boulder wall,
Towers a windy promontory there,
The most exlated windy rock of all
And in the bracing blowing air
I mount the lenches [shelves of rock] stair by stair,
And hear the wind like waves upon the shore
Rush in the heath and in the fissures roar.

And back on the unchanging Flat of Stoke
Stand rugged stones in circle, whence the sun
The whole of day was seen, and where the stroke
Of sacrifice was at his rising done.
And out on Ramsley's brackened floor,
And high on Eyam's black barren moor,
And far o'er Offerton and all around
These olden temples stud the higher ground.

As mete it is; O hillmen here that knew
To hery in high places like to these,
Surely such instinct it was high and true;
Believing do I bow upon my knees.
Before I loved the written Word
Bare rock and sky my spirit stirred
To deism: at flooding of the day
Blindly, and like some poor dumb beast, I pray.

There is a lonely bay within the edge,
High rocks it has like huge hieratic doors,
A low rock in the centre on the ledge,
Above the heaven, below the valley floors.
Our blood is of that early brood,
Uncivilized, untamed, and crude:
I know for all the cultured vales beneath,
Here is my element and here my breath.

Perhaps best known for her children's stories about Little Grey Rabbit, Little Red Fox, *and* Sam Pig, *Alison Uttley was the author of more than a hundred books. Born in Cromford and brought up in rural Derbyshire, she was educated at the Lea School in Holloway and Lady Manners School in Bakewell, where she developed a love for science which led to a scholarship to Manchester University to read physics.*

Alison began writing to support herself and her son after she was widowed in 1930. Her first and most famous books were the series of tales about animals, but she later wrote for older children and adults, particularly focussing on rural topics, notably in The Country Child *(1931), a fictionalised account of her childhood experiences at her family farm, Castletop, near Cromford, and* A Traveller in Time *(1939), which was based on the plot, by Anthony Babington of nearby Dethick, to free Mary Queen of Scots from Wingfield Manor in the sixteenth century.*

The following excerpt is from The Farm on the Hill, *published in 1941, where Susan is taken to see the view from Carlton Pastures – which are actually above Bakewell and from where in reality, not even the keenest eye could see the Welsh hills or the sea.*

ALISON UTTLEY *The Farm on the Hill* (1941)

THE OUTING

'This is the pasture,' said Nell, as they climbed a long steep grassy hill. It was full of hummocks and dips, and the trees growing there were stunted and wind-swept. It was a disappointing field, with no flowers or water-troughs, but at the top there was the view. Other people were climbing too, which astonished Susan, to whom a field was a private possession.

From the summit they looked over a wide stretch of country.

A thousand fields lay below them, a pattern of green and brown falling to the vast plain and rising from the hyacinth-blue hills of Wales. On the horizon gleamed the sea, a pale silver band of light, fairy and remote as if it were a stream in heaven's fields. Between that romantic vision and the hill-top were countless little woods, rounded like balls, with here a cluster of cottages, and there a church steeple pointed to the clouds. The whole green cup in the hills was radiantly alive, the air quivered with light, the middle distance was so clear that the girls could distinguish cattle in the infinitesimal squares and oblongs like the animals in a toy scene. They pointed out the nearer farms, speaking of the men who lived there, excited as they told each other of a field ploughed or grassland turned to wheat. Pasture and meadow, ploughland and wood were all known to them, and they stored away their birds-eye peep to tell their brothers all the news. Susan stared at the jolly little haystacks, the stone farms, glittering like pebbles, the ponds like mirrors, the red carts and tiny figures, each one a home with kitchen and dairy and barn, such as she knew, and perhaps a girl like herself living and playing and growing up, but strangers for always. Then she raised her eyes to the dim hills, blue and violet and lavender-grey, an unknown country, six counties, spread out like a patchwork quilt under the sky.

5.
FORGIVE US OUR TRESPASSERS

It could be said that the beginnings of the outdoor movement were right here in the Peak. Certainly this is where the sport of rock climbing began at the turn of the twentieth century, and the lure of the Dark Peak moorlands was a keen enticement to the workers in the grim cotton mills of Manchester and steel works of Sheffield, for they were so close they could see them from their back-to-back terraced homes.

But most of those moors were forbidden territory until the coming of the Peak District National Park in 1951. After the Enclosure Acts of the late eighteenth and nineteenth centuries much of what was once common land was appropriated by landowners mainly for grouse shooting, and the public was excluded.

The situation was vividly described by Hayfield's Luke Garside in his booklet Kinder Scout, with the Footpaths and Bridle roads about Hayfield, *published in 1880.*

LUKE GARSIDE *Kinder Scout, with the Footpaths and Bridle roads about Hayfield* (1880)

A great part of Kinder Scout and the adjoining moors were, until lately, what is known as 'King's Land', over which the public might ramble at their pleasure; but about the year 1830 the whole of these lands were surveyed, and allotted to the various owners of contiguous lands, according to the size of their holdings. No allotment, however, as far as we know, was made to the poor, or for their benefit; and it seems that since this time more than forty acres of what was known as 'Poor Man's Wood,' have disappeared from many modern maps.

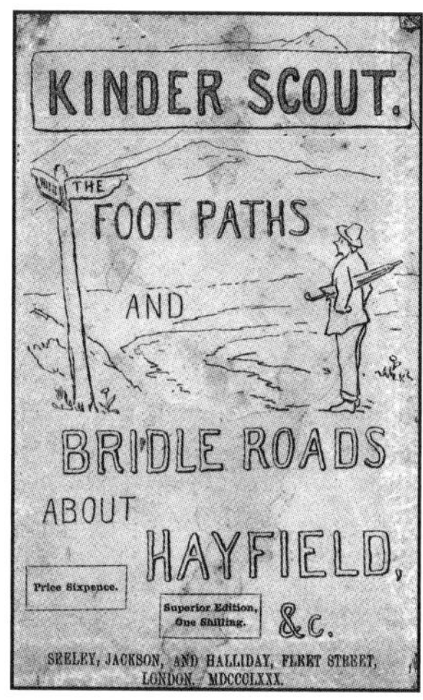

Luke Garside's 1880 Kinder Scout guidebook

Garside tabulated the subsequent award of land as follows:

> To the rich, according to their riches: 2000 acres
> To the poor, according to their poverty: 0 acres
> Moreover, minus upwards of: 40 acres

At this time, there was not the same distinction between rock climbers and cavers or pot-holers as there is today. Those early explorers were just as keen on delving into the caves and caverns of the limestone country of the White Peak as they were on clinging to the gritstone edges of the Dark Peak.

This first account is of a winter trespass across then-forbidden Kinder Scout from E.A. Baker's classic turn-of-the-twentieth-century account of early walking and climbing in the Peak, Moors, Crags and Caves of the High Peak. *Like many others at the time, Baker was as much a caver as climber.*

E.A. BAKER *Moors, Crags and Caves of the High Peak* (1903)

WINTER DAYS ON KINDER SCOUT

> The time seems near, if it has not actually arrived, when the chastened sublimity of a moor, a sea, or a mountain will be all of nature that is absolutely in keeping with the moods of the more thinking among mankind.
>
> – *The Return of the Native* by Thomas Hardy

A characteristic of Peak scenery endearing it to the hardy rambler is that it loses nothing of its peculiar glory in winter. Right in the centre of England, midway between Sheffield and Manchester, at the threshold of the world's most populous cluster of manufacturing towns, there lies this broad area of wild country, as lone and untamed as any south of Cheviot. Through the factory smoke and the steam we have glimpses, now and again, of the dark line of the edges. Even business is lightened a little by the knowledge that an hour or two might take us clean away, on to a heathery moor that wears the same harsh, impassable face it wore when Britain was peopled by savages.

Whether it be, as Thomas Hardy maintains so eloquently, that these austere landscapes, whose prophecy is as sombre as their history, are naturally in harmony with our modern pessimism, or that they exercise a tonic influence upon our pampered and jaded minds; or whether it be merely the physical sense of space and freedom, or the suggestions of the mysterious and the illimitable with which the shadowy expanses and the dark ravines sway the imagination as with the suggestiveness of poetry; true it is that the gloomy scenes which our grandfathers hated, draw us with a subtle and a powerful spell.

Winter is most in keeping with such scenery. Then the gaunt crags, bristling along the edges of the moorlands, loom through veils of cloud that transfigure and idealise; the withered heather is susceptible of all the tints flung upon it by the vagaries of the sunlight; and the tracts of coarse grass, embrowned and burnt red by frost, are changed through a hundred gradations of warm, rich colour. Winter, again, with storms and flooded cloughs, with deep snow-wreaths, ice-clad rocks, and bewildering mists, affords the incorrigible wanderer a little of the adventure for which he is ready to travel much farther afield.

Peakland scenery culminates in Kinder Scout, to which, by a confusion of ideas, the Ordnance Surveyors gave the name of a whole district.

Unabashed by its flatness, they called it the Peak. In a number of places the Scout rises above the 2,000ft level; it has the noblest crags, the biggest peat-moss, and the finest waterfall in the district. Its waters run to the eastern and western seas, the cloughs that penetrate to the heart of it are like mountain corries, with turbulent streams rushing to the dales. And Kinder Scout in winter is as wild a place as any mountain in England or Wales. To cross it is no less of an adventure than to cross Scawfell (sic) under like conditions, and the grandeur and novelty of the experience repay one quite as well.

My first ascent of the Scout was made years ago during a winter of memorable severity. For long weeks the deep drifts were sealed up with frost; many sheep and cattle perished; the wild things were, like the hares, slain in hundreds, or driven like the grouse to seek the abodes of man and pick up a living with the domestic fowls; lines were blocked, mail-carts snowed up, and several people were caught and overcome in the storms.

Our party of four came to the new station at Edale, accoutred for the fray. Wild indeed was the scene that opened on us when we emerged from Totley Tunnel. The dales with their pine woods, black and gaunt, set against the snow-slopes; the dark crags high aloft, the 'cornices'of snow along the ridges; and the dark-brown, heaving Derwent, swirling along sombrely below, altogether made a thoroughly highland picture. Most imposing was the lofty cirque immuring the head of Edale; Mam Tor, Lord's Seat, and Cowburn, rising up and up until their white slopes melted, with no visible line of contour, into the whiteness of the mist.

No sooner had we left the hamlet of Edale Chapel and the homestead at the foot of Grindsbrook Clough, than we found ourselves entering a very Arctic world. A half-obliterated cart-road led through a spinney to the open moor. Down the middle of the deep, rugged clough ran the Grindsbrook, if it could be said to run when the springs were congealed, and all the cascades stricken into stalactites of greenish-blue ice. To right

Winter walking on Kinder Scout

and left stretched long slopes of snow up to the clouds, the head of the clough was full of whirling mist that boded trouble, and hundreds of feet above our heads the sharp end of Ringing Rocher [Roger] towered like a graceful curving horn, off which the gale blew puffs of snow-dust like smoke. What a change from the manifold shades of colour, and more, from the concert of descending streams, that make this clough delightful in summer! The bottom was heaped up with drifts that made each step a muscular effort, and the careful pioneering of two alpenstocks did not save us from many a tumble into bog-holes filled with snow.

Tired with the slow progression, two of us left the neighbourhood of the stream, and struggled up the fell-side towards the looming cliffs of Upper Tor. Since the snow was being continually blown down the hill, the higher we went the harder grew the surface, and therewithal the more slippery. Steps had to be kicked one by one with our hobnailed toes most of the way up, and a slip would have sent us on a long, swift slide. Not far up, a flock of grouse numbering several hundreds went off complaining, and we found many cup-shaped hollows in the snow, where these unfortunates had been spending the night. The last bit of climbing was up a couloir between two high buttresses of grit, and then we were on the top.

Where were the other pair, who had chosen to cut their way right up to the ice-bound gorge of the Grindsbrook? They were lost to sight in the misty gulf beneath us, across which we looked to the long snow-slope of Grindsbrook Knoll. The vast sheet of white was not unrelieved by zones and patches of shading, the buried heather marked the snow with a delicate etching, and every undulation changed the character of the surface. Areas of unsullied white bordered on areas of grey, and the frozen snow had been diapered by the graver of the sleet-laden wind to multitudinous patterns. Over every watercourse the upper snow curved like a wave; and on every hill-brow the cornice, several feet wide, and whole furlongs in length, was a startling proof of the cohesiveness and plasticity of this product of the clouds. In one place we trespassed on the cornice, and nearly went through into the deep ravine at the head of the clough. The walking was a good deal better than it would have been in summer, the bog being covered with a hard pavement, very different from the soft snow near the dale. Instead of the 'groughs' full of inky water and mud, we had arches of snow and wind-fretted canopies, under which there was shelter from the tolerable blast.

Now we caught sight of our comrades nearing the edge. One was cutting steps up the frozen slope with ice-axe, and evidently selecting the most 'sporting' route. A burst of sunshine shot through just then, and illumined the whole length of the deep, winding clough, touching the ridge beyond Edale with soft gold, and suffusing with roseate hues the pale wisps and wreaths mist that floated in the gulf beneath us. We made gallant attempt to get the camera into action, but the flying clouds

Kinder Downfall, from Luke Garside's 1880 guide

shut out the picture before our numbed fingers had fixed it up. Then, after lunching comfortlessly under the lea of a big rock, we set off nor'-nor'-west, the leader marching at the head of the file, compass in hand. Once only the mist lifted a moment, and Hey Ridge with its tors beyond the Ashop glimmered and vanished.

By some mistake we came out on the edge of Crowden Clough, a long and dreary way from the Downfall, and someone uttered the fatal suggestion that we might go down here. As yet we had made but a half-hearted attempt to cross the Scout to Kinder Downfall; yet no one felt the spirit of protest, all had had enough. We stood on the edge of just such another steep slope, covered with hard snow, as the one we had ascended with so much toil and trouble. A glissade was proposed.

Three of us had only read about that thrilling Alpine game, and we trembled; glissading, we understood, played terrible havoc with beginners. When, however, our captain shot off gracefully down the giddy incline, steering a course easily and confidently with the handle of his ice-axe, a second followed timidly, and now all four had taken the plunge. Sitting with legs firmly advanced, the surface snow collecting under us in a kind of natural sled, we were off like toboggans, with so little sense of friction we might have been shooting through air. But our steering was inadequate; to handle a long alpenstock as rudder needs practice. We rocketed off sideways, on our backs and on our faces, finishing with a wild plunge into the drifts at the bottom. Who shall describe the exhilarating thrill of that first mad rush? We were almost tempted to re-ascend and begin again.

And after our long trudge back through miles of drifts, after dinner at the Nag's Head, one enthusiast, drunk with the charms of glissading, borrowed a tea-tray, and beguiled the twilight hour with startling evolutions on the snow, not more to his own delectation than to the joy and wonder of the villagers.

It was winter yet in the upper regions, though in the dales it was a hot day in spring, when I got my first glimpse of the Downfall and the glories of Kinder's western edges. On this occasion, it may as well be confessed, I had not armed myself with a licence to view these carefully treasured landscapes; but trusting partly to sound legs and lungs, and partly to the known frailties of keepers, I had deliberately committed the sin of trespassing. Howbeit, in those days, before the famous controversy as to the right of way over Mill Hill, the crime was not a heinous one, if you consider how wide a stretch of superb country was nominally forbidden to the public.

Having gotten a long way up the Kinder stream from Hayfield without let or hindrance, I was suddenly aware of two figures striding rapidly along the hillside at the distance of several fields above me. Obviously they were bent on meeting me at a point farther up the brook. At the next wall, therefore, the highest on this side, I took the precaution to change my direction, and creeping uphill to the left under its cover, I found myself, after a tough pull, on the open moor, with nothing near me but a few sheep and many scores of startled grouse, that whirred almost from beneath my feet, with a noise that I thought would attract the enemy. But so far as they were concerned I had slipped away into the mist, and I saw them no more.

This unpremeditated digression took me to the north end of the Scout, where a long, dark edge stretches east, crowned at intervals with oddly-shaped stacks and towers of swarthy grit. My way was south, along the western edge, to the Downfall, a mile away. As I skirted the crags, ness after ness jutted out from the long, mountainous escarpment into the golden haze that shut out the world; and, in the deep bays and coves between, late fields of snow gleamed in the shadow and glistened in the sun. The russet hues and ruddy gold of the grass patches covered the fell-side with warm colour, and where Nab Brow loomed dimly through the haze, seemed to stain the very air and the sunshine. Never did the Witch's [now known as the Mermaid's] Pool look more visionary – a patch of flashing blue, ethereal as a patch of sky. Then the black gorge of the Downfall opened beneath me, but the fall itself was shrunk to a jet pellucid water flinging prismatic tints on the crags that enfold it.

The dread of keepers was still in my soul, and without halting to eat the coveted sandwich I pushed on up the main stream, now merely a chain of pools issuing from a tunnel beneath thick beds of snow. The two of these, for the snow was hard and firm, offered the most convenient path, far better than the humpy moss hags to right and left; and I went south-east and north-east, up one stream and down another, till I was safely across the bog. Then in a nook of Fairbrook Clough, the combe that descends through fold after heathery fold of the great hillside to the Ashop, with rillet of snow-fed water spurting deliciously from a fall hard by, I ate my belated lunch.

A winter ascent of Kinder Scout has now become an annual institution. But we have not always found the great fall buried in ice and snow. The

Kinder Downfall, from the cover of the Handbook of the Manchester Ramblers' Federation, 1925

Scout is perhap at its worst during a mild winter, as on one December day when we saw it in a storm. There had been a fall of snow, but heavy rains had swollen the Kinder stream to a roaring torrent. In the upper region outlines of cliff and watercourse faded imperceptibly into the mist, all accurate measures of size and altitude were abolished, so that as the water came down out of the unseen and foamed over the rocks before being engulfed in the gloom below, we could almost imagine ourselves gazing on the fume and turmoil of a Norwegian foss. The Downfall was magnificent, for a hurricane was blowing sheer against the spot where nearly 2,000ft above sea-level, it plunges over the crag. The instant the stream touched the brink it was caught by the gale, with the effect, often seen in the mountains, that the water was hurled upwards bodily in a white column, whilst in the lulls of the blast it dashed hither and thither, as if directed from place to place by some mighty hand, drenching the rocks with spray. The tortured stream raged and leapt like a furious animal. It seemed a living thing.

Two of us found an easy passage up the cliff, but the others got into difficulties, and did not reach the top for some time. We two might have been standing on a rock-bound coast, staring into the surf and rack of a storm. The uproar drowned our voices. Eyes could not pierce the weltering mist, the roar of many waters came up from below, the wind bellowed in the rents and hollows of the cliff, and every streamlet as it tumbled over the edge was blown aloft like the spray from a blow-hole, and driven furiously over the face of the moor.

When the missing scramblers appeared, we set off across the bog, up the river-bed for nearly a mile, and then, by the compass, over the watershed to the Fairbrook. To steer a way across this wilderness of quaking bogs, deep and slippery water-channels, and thick-set humps of peaty earth, is one of the severest tests of a man's ability to use the compass. He is bound to consult the needle at every few yards, for to take many steps together in anything like a straight line is impossible; one simply blunders on among the gullies and ridges, and corrects one's aberrations from time to time. On a clear day it is bad enough; but when we are immersed in a current of thick, soaking mist, and the fluid bog is more fluid than ever, all our faculties must be on the alert to save us from utter bewilderment.

The anniversary of that day has been celebrated by a long series of rambles over the Scout. Sometimes we have found the Downfall entirely frozen up, a sheet of crystal flung in translucent folds across the rugged wall. But once again we encountered weather as uncomfortable as that just described. Among the dozen in our party were several who perhaps had never been on a peat-moss in their lives, and certainly never in any but the finest summer weather. They had heard great tales about Kinder Scout in winter, and were ambitious to see the highest spot in their county under the grandest conditions. At Hayfield it was not exactly fine, yet not rainy; by the time we had passed the Downfall we were nearly as wet as if we had climbed straight through it.

An account by walking author and inveterate trespasser Thomas L. Tudor, of an illicit trip to Kinder Downfall, and an early description of the celebrated 'blow-back' phenomenon, when westerly winds reverse the flow of the waterfall.

THOMAS L. TUDOR *The High Peak to Sherwood* (1926)

At certain times of the year it is possible to cross the plateau of Kinder without doing appreciable damage to the shooting rights. But it as well to obtain a permit, and so provide against unpleasant interviews with keepers. The expedition, however, is not suited to the mere rambler. Certain ways up and down are distinctly dangerous, and the terrible wildness of the top, its deep and slimy peat-holes, its swamps and tangled vegetation, and its pathless solitudes, make an appeal only to very special temperaments. The stony barriers that surround the plateau, almost at a uniform level of just over 2,000 feet, have kept the edges higher than the interior and to invade its midst is to lose sight of all the surrounding world, and to see no directing landmarks in the valleys below. After several crossings you may pick out the contours if the day be propitious, but like a navigator, you had better be prepared to steer by the heavens and the compass.

Along with Bleaklow to the north, Kinder sustains its title to a place in the Pennine Range by the fact that it sheds its waters east and west, to the Derwent and the Mersey. The Downfall flows west, Fairbrook and the streams on that side flow east. Sometimes on the high moor you may see the tiny rivulets meandering through the peaty ground, two or three close together, and hardly showing any difference in their direction. But one is on its way to the North Sea, the other to the Irish Channel. The neck of the moor between Fairbrook and the Downfall would seem to be the least likely place where the direction would be lost, but in this region more than one fatality has occurred.

The edges give by far the most thrilling sensations, and if you have ankles of steel so much the better for getting along through their savage confusion. Perhaps the most superb viewpoint is Fairbrook Naze, and the edge of the Fairbrook waterfall. But the region of the Downfall has, in itself, a wild beauty that excels all other places on the actual top. Here the Kinder River has cut its main bed, wide and rock-strewn, through the peat hillocks, and flows, gathering in many tributary waters, flashing and foaming here, spreading like a mirror there, and so pouring its clear burden to the final fall through a stupendous confusion of tumbled cliffs. While the finest effects depend, of course, on a wet season, it is seldom that the stream along the high ground is not a picture of wild and animated beauty. But when the heather hangs purple over the waters, and the blue sky sleeps in the pools, there is hardly any scene more perfect. Yet if you should chance to be there when the Downfall is blowing back in the sunlight, and the sunbows leap through the spray, that indeed is your perfect moment, for the rush and whirl of the mist, and the fairy dancing of the iris on its crest make a scene that Nature herself only rises to in her rarest moods. The cliffs that enclose the Downfall are in reality the true Kinderscout, though the name is generally given to the entire table-land. Kinder is a name that baffles etymologists, but it is probably a British name signifying a headland, and 'Scout' is surely what it looks like, an old Romance word meaning 'to watch'.

The discovery of a fabulous hoard of Saxon jewellery and coins in a cave in Beeston Tor in the Manifold Valley was made by the caver, the Rev. George H. Wilson of Bakewell, in 1924. This is his account of that famous find as related in his booklet, Some Caves and Crags of Peakland, *published two years later.*

GEORGE H. WILSON *Some Caves and Crags of Peakland* (1926)

Interest in the cave had waned or died when, after the war, I was able to follow up and test a fixed idea that British and Saxon refugees had dwelt in this place during times of invasion. The Saxon Chronicles and other sources for our knowledge of the period gave hints of valuables hurriedly removed when the fierce Danish invader appeared. During the Spring and Summer of 1924, brief periods of leisure allowed the clue to be followed up. Those who were asked to accompany me on various visits either lacked time or taste for the work. Some of those lonely adventures in that abode of suggested horrors were deeply interesting . . . On September 17th I went to the cave alone. The day was a soaker, and on reaching Holme End by bus, there being no train, the four miles down the valley were done on foot in pouring rain. The river was in flood, and the last stretch from Grindon station was over the short cut through dripping brushwood. Soaked upper garments were left to drain in the first chamber while I pushed on into an inner recess where some difficult work went forward for about six hours. After about three hours a beautiful Saxon brooch turned up, proving that the clue followed through the years had not led me astray. Coins of Burgred and Alfred the Great came next, so well preserved that their inscriptions could be read in the light of my lamp. Then a massive gold ring shone up in the acetylene glare, and a quantity of gold wire which had evidently been woven into a braid with material which had long since perished. Other coins were appearing when a glance at my watch proved that no time must be lost if the last train up the valley was to be caught. The night could have been spent in the cave if food and dry clothing had been available, and friends in Buxton acquainted. The hoard was hurriedly examined and packed. Thirty-six coins of various Saxon kings, a very fine circular brooch, a circlet of gold, and many strands of gold wire.

Evidently the items had lain there undisturbed since some refugee in the time of Alfred hid them in a day of trouble.

Patrick Monkhouse was the highly respected deputy and later northern editor of the Manchester Guardian *for forty years, and like many of 'staffers' at that time, was a keen rambler and explorer of the Peak. His 1932 book* On Foot in the Peak *was a masterpiece of outdoor writing and in my opinion remains one of the best walking books on the Peak District ever written. In this excerpt from his introduction, he explains why the area should always be called 'the Peak' rather than 'the Peak District'.*

PATRICK MONKHOUSE *On Foot in the Peak* (1932)

The Peak is a district, not a mountain. Therefore I have called this booklet 'On Foot in the Peak' and not 'in the Peak District'.

The belief of the ordnance surveyors that the mountain, which most people call loosely Kinder Scout, is correctly called 'The Peak' seems to me to be based on a false deduction.

In Elizabeth's days there was no doubt about it. Old Camden, who did for the London of his day what the American cameramen do for us, exploring Derbyshire as they do Darkest Africa, describes it fully enough. He came up from the south, by Derby. 'The west part beyond Derwent,' he says, 'which they call the Peake, rich in lead, iron and coales – also feedeth sheep very commodiously.' Iron ore is not mined in the Peak proper, but coal is raised (or used to be at that time) about the headwaters of the Goyt and the Dane, a long way west of the Derwent. Camden, then, clearly indicates the whole of this territory by 'the Peake'.

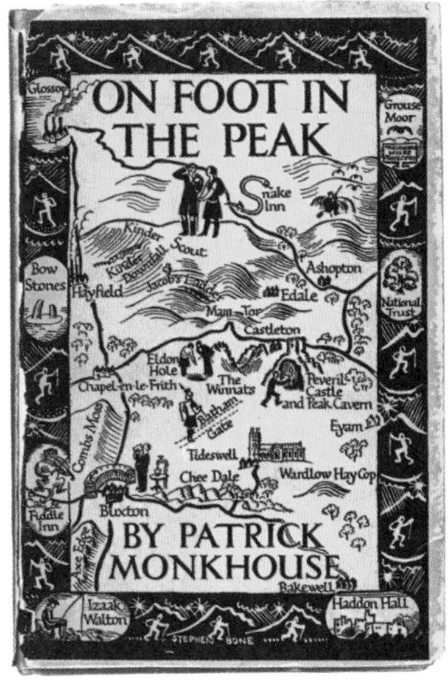

On Foot in the Peak

A little later he writes, 'it was called in the old English tongue *Peac-lond*, and at this day the Peake'. Most place-names in this country are Anglo-Saxon, and in Anglo-Saxon the whole country was 'Peakland', that is, 'the land of peaks' not 'the land of the Peak'. (As when we say Lakeland, we mean the land of lakes, not of a particular lake.)

One or two points in corroboration; Michael Drayton, who did the same sort of thing as Camden, in verse but on the whole less poetically, describes the Peak as

> A withered bedlam long, with bleared waterish eyes
> As proud of her leadmines as others of their corn.

In Charles Cotton's addendum to *The Compleat Angler*, the traveller, asking for ale, says, 'it is not right that a man should come from London to drink wine in the Peak'. The inn at which he is drinking is the Talbot at Ashbourne.

Let it rest at that. The Peak went on being called the Peak until Dr Johnson brought out his dictionary. He defined a peak as 'a sharply pointed hill'. He should have known better. He had been at least as far as Ashbourne. He did infinite harm. People coming up from the south began to look for a properly defined Peak and could not find one, so they fastened the name quite improperly on to the highest hill they could find, a great flat tableland which hitherto had not enjoyed a name at all

– or rather, had many names, for the people in every valley round about had their own names for what part of it was visible to them.

Once 'the Peak' is down on a map as a mountain, the bastard phrase 'Peak District' follows easily enough. I must beg the railway companies' pardon for reverting to the original form, and note in passing the curious fact that the latest edition of Mr Baddeley's 'Thorough Guide', published in 1908 – and excellent book, out of print now, but you can often get a copy second hand – has 'The Peak' in gold letters on its ruddy face, and 'Peak District' on the back. Mr Baddeley's thoroughness has evidently prompted him, where doubt lay, to give both forms.

And there is – I must admit it in honesty – one fair reason for saying 'Peak District', namely that the Peak is a district but not the whole of the district which is called the Peak District. Thus one might conceivably talk about the Snowdonia district, meaning the district round Snowdon and the district round that again. Old Camden – my faithful stand-by – first struck the Pennine Chain in Staffordshire. It runs, he says, 'like as Apennine in Itlay, through the middest of England, with a continued ridge, rising more and more with continued tops and cliffs one after another ever as far as Scotland. Here they are called "Mooreland", after a while the Peake, Blackstone Edge, the Craven, the Stainmore and at length Cheviot.' Here the Peak (and curiously Blackstone Edge above Rochdale) is clearly referred to as a chain of hills, not as an individual hill. But it is distinguished from the Staffordshire 'Moorelands', that is the wild country above Leek, and dominated by the Roaches and by the long bulk of Morridge. This country I have included under the general title of the Peak, and thus have confessedly strayed over the border line of strict propriety. The district described in this little book is, in fact, pretty well all or any of the hill country, south of the pass by which the main road from Manchester to Huddersfield goes, by way of the 'Isle of Syke'. It comprises Derbyshire (in bulk), Yorkshire (in small quantities), a big corner of Staffordshire and much more of Cheshire than most people think. Lancashire just pokes a nose into the country – the old hill fort of Bucton Castle above Mossley is in Lancashire – but otherwise plays no part in the scenery. Lancashire's part in recent years has been to provide people to look at the scenery. As Meredith said,

> Earth was not earth, until her sons appeared,
> Nor beauty beauty, ere young love was born –

on which principle the charms of the Peak have in recent years gained very much (contrary to the opinion of superior and exclusive persons) from the thousands of young people who have come out from Manchester and Sheffield and other big towns to enjoy clean air and hard exercise in the country.

Monkhouse later disparages the use of the word 'hiking' and describes the extrordinary mass weekend exodus from Manchester to the hills of the Peak. In the very year of the Kinder Mass Trespass, he also gives some handy hints for would-be trespassers, of which he was undoubtedly one.

A minor outcome of the movement to 'stay the night' is that it would give meaning – the right meaning – to the much misused word – 'hike'. 'Hiking' is an American word, with a proper meaning of its own. It means going from one sleeping-place to another and carrying one's gear with one. A man on what used to be, and still should be, called a walking tour may properly be said to hike. A man who catches the train home does not. The word has swept into general use for lack of a rival. 'Rambling' is so inapt a word for the stiff twenty miles which many ramblers take in their stride. I prefer to stick to walking as a general term, but I do not bar (though I do not love) 'hiking' when used in the right sense.

But it must be conceded that grim necessity compels these many one-day mountaineers to catch the train home, and one must be thankful for the train and bus services which make it possible for the young men and maidens of Sheffield and Manchester and other big smoky cities to snatch a few hours in the hills. The movement which has brought young townsfolk out on to the moors has hardly a parallel elsewhere in Britain. For an hour on Sunday mornings it looks like Bank Holiday in the Manchester stations, except that families do not go to Blackpool for Whit-week in shorts. South-countrymen gasp to look at it.

There are people, living in the country, or older visitors to it, who deplore this movement, or, if not the movement as a whole, some of its devotees. And it must be frankly admitted that the week-end swarm includes some who have not yet learned to harmonise their manners with rural scenery. They sing tunelessly, and argue in loud voices, and strum on stringed instruments, complains the old-timer, and hints that those who sing the loudest, and dress the most strangely, have not ventured more than a few miles from a railway station.

This last charge is easily answered. A good deal, though not all, of the distinction between the 'true rambler' and the 'noisy hooligans' is fictitious. I have met with people making a very raucous noise in some very considerable hills, not to be reached without dust and sweat, and I fancy that most of those whose behaviour offends simple quiet people have done a sturdy fifteen miles or so in the course of the day.

I am not going to quarrel with these lusty recruits of the game. Times will teach them how to be at peace with the hills, as quickly as any reproof of yours or mine. After six days spent in the workshop, or perched on an office stool, with a choice between whispers and silence, not wonder if they find, in the freedom from walls and roofs, freedom from other restrictions and bonds which lap them round in everyday life. The one day in the country is so very unlike the six days in the town that the blood rushes to your head . . . There is not better way to cool it than to stay in the country overnight. To walk into the pure Derbyshire morning takes away all desire to howl. It takes your breath away.

. . . I am not going to discuss the ethics of trespassing, or of grouse-shooting, or of private property, or of the Access to Mountains Bill. The fact that a particular route is described in the following pages does not necessarily imply that there is a right of way, or that I have recommended you to follow it. All I want to do in this paragraph is to indicate which walks are trespassing and which are not. Then, if you are a firm believer in the rights of property, you can take care to keep off them. If not, you can take the usual precautions.

Later, as Monkhouse describes the route across the western shoulder of Kinder Scout between South Head and Mount Famine, he gives some useful, if lighthearted, advice for would-be trespassers.

From this point there is a well known and useful cut across the moor, about 1¾ miles, to Edale Cross. There is a faint path, but no right of way, and on populous Sundays a gamekeeper may be seen sitting with a dog and a gun on the side of South Head. His presence is usually an adequate deterrent, and the gun has not yet been used.

He also gives some useful tips for walking across the endless peat bogs of the Dark Peak moors, which will instantly be recognised by ardent 'bogtrotters'.

These groughs (drainage channels in the peat) are the bane of the easy, the joy of the tough walker. You follow the heathery ridges between them as far as you can, and then jump, to land as high up as you can on the opposite side, and a quick slither takes you up to the next ridge. You soon get the trick, but it is heavy going. When the groughs run in the right direction, it is often easier to walk in the bed of them; but you must keep your eye on the compass, for you will see no landmarks while you are in them. In the summer, when the sun and wind have dried the mud, the experts put on rubber shoes and glide nimbly over the groughs, to their own delight and the despair of perspiring gamekeepers.

Ewan MacColl, then known by his birth name of Jimmy Miller, took part as a youngster in the Mass Trespass in 1932, and his song, 'The Manchester Rambler', has become firmly identified with it, and an anthem for northern ramblers. Note the final line of the chorus given here: 'But I am a free man on Sunday', is the original, 1932, version. His widow, the American folk singer Peggy Seeger, explained to me that Ewan later changed the words to the more politically correct: 'But I have my freedom on Sunday' As Peggy recounts in The Essential Ewan MacColl Songbook *(Oak Publications, 2001): 'Ewan quite liked the new line once he got used to it.'*

EWAN MACCOLL 'The Manchester Rambler' (1932)

I've been over Snowdon, I've slept upon Crowden,
I've camped by the Wain Stones as well;
I've sunbathed on Kinder, been burned to a cinder,
And many more things I can tell.

My rucksack has oft been my pillow.
The heather has oft been my bed;
And sooner than part from the mountains
I think I would rather be dead.

I'm a rambler, I'm a rambler from Manchester way,
I get all my pleasure the hard moorland way;
I may be a wage slave on Monday
But I am a free man on Sunday.

There's pleasure in dragging through peat bogs and bragging
Of all the fine walks that you know;
There's even a measure of some kind of pleasure
In wading through ten feet of snow.
I've stood on the edge of the Downfall,
And seen all the valleys outspread;
And sooner than part from the mountains,
I think I would rather be dead. [Chorus]

The day was just ending as I was descending
Down Grindsbrook just by Upper Tor,
When a voice cried, 'Hey you!' in the way keepers do
(He'd the worst face that ever I saw).
The things that he said were unpleasant;
In the teeth of his fury I said,
'Sooner than part from the mountains,
'I think I would rather be dead.' [Chorus]

He called me a louse and said, 'Think of the grouse.'
Well I thought but I still couldn't see

Why old Kinder Scout and the moors round about
Couldn't take both the poor grouse and me.
He said, 'All this land is my master's.'
At that I stood shaking my head;
No man has the right to own mountains
Any more than the deep ocean bed. [Chorus]

I once loved a maid, a spot-welder by trade,
She was fair as the rowan in bloom,
And the blue of her eye matched the June moorland sky,
And I wooed her from April to June.
On the day that we should have been married,
I went for a ramble instead,
For sooner than part from the mountains,
I think I would rather be dead. [Chorus]

So I'll walk where I will over mountain and hill
And I'll lie where the bracken is deep;
I belong to the mountains, the clear running fountains
Where the grey rocks rise rugged and steep.
I've seen the white hare in the gulleys,
And the curlew fly high overhead,
And sooner than part from the mountains
I think I would rather be dead. [Chorus]

Another, lesser-known Ewan MacColl song associated with the treasured rambling days of his youth in Salford was 'Mass Trespass 1932', which was sung to the traditional Scottish tune of 'The Road to the Isles'.

EWAN MACCOLL 'Mass Trespass 1932'

We are young workers who in search of healthy sport
Leave Manchester each weekend for a hike.
Though the best moorland in Derbyshire is closed
To us we'll ramble where we like.

For by Kinder and by Bleaklow and through all the Goyt we'll go,
We'll ramble over mountain, moor and fen;
And we'll fight against the trespass laws for every rambler's rights
And trespass over Kinder Scout again.

For the mass trespass is the only way there is
To gain access to the mountains once again.

John Derry's Across the Derbyshire Moors *was, and still is, another classic in Peak District outdoor literature. It went through many editions after its first publication by Loxley Brothers in 1934 at the height of the trespassing craze. The first editions had a splendid drawing (pictured opposite) of a gentleman wearing pince-nez, a Norfolk jacket and plus-fours on the cover and advertisements inside for Newsholme's Corn Cure and stout walking boots.*

Derry was a Sheffield JP and a former editor of the Sheffield Independent. *Later editions of* Across the Derbyshire Moors *were published by the* Sheffield Telegraph *and revised by G.H.B. Ward, the 'King' of the famous Sheffield Clarion Ramblers.*

JOHN DERRY *Across the Derbyshire Moors* (1934)

TO BACK TOR

The walk from Strines Lane end to Strines Inn is pleasantly undulating. You can see the ragged face of Back Tor, your destination, on the left front, the most distant of the roughnesses on the long summit of Derwent Edge. The moor immediately left of you is Strines Edge, and the county boundary, which has come down from Stanage Edge along the green 'Moscar Cross Road' that passes between Moscar Cross and Moscar Lodge, and crosses our road at Sugworth Lane end, follows this Edge, and then strikes up Derwent Moor to Dovestone Tor – the highest summit on the actual face of Derwent Edge.

As we near Strines Inn, Bradfield Dale opens out on the right prettily, with the whole of Strines Reservoir (finished in 1871) and Dale Dike Reservoir (1875) visible. Strines Inn, by the way, was the hall or home of the Worralls in the mid-sixteenth century or earlier, and the Worrall arms are over the doorway.

Cover of the 8th edition of Across the Derbyshire Moors (1918)

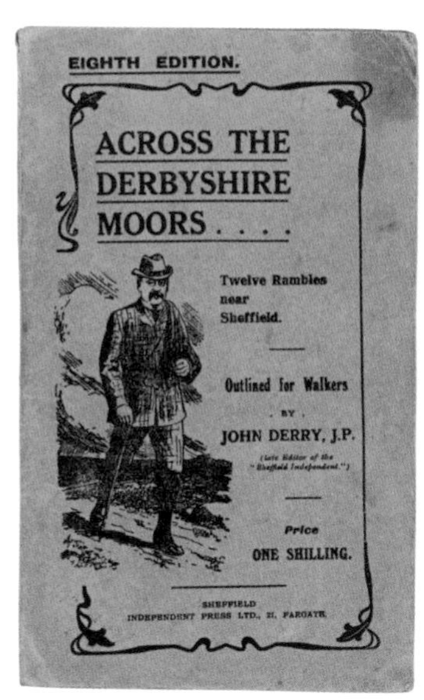

Just beyond the Inn the road begins a sharp descent to the Strines brook. At the top of the slope on the right is a wayside stone bearing the words 'Take off'. It marks the place where 'chain' horses were taken off after helping up the hill. The Strines Dike at the bottom now has a stone bridge which replaces the little wooden bridge and the earlier stepping stones or strides, which are said to have originated the name Strines.

The Peak District and NCFPS (the Peak and Northern Footpath Preservation Society) placed a sign post here, and at the Abbey Cottage end of Green Sitches track, etc., in 1933–4. The Enclosure Act gives 60 feet of public road as far as the parish boundary at Bradfield Gate Head. After passing the first stream (there is another – Hollingdale Brook – a little further on) turn sharply to the left, and ascend by a cart road which leads rather steeply up through a wide, open space between walls, with woods beyond the walls. It is worth while to look back, for the Strines Reservoir nestles brightly in its wood-clothed basin.

When at a gateway you reach the open moor, the 'keeper''s house at Foulstone Delf is just before you. Leave it on your left and follow the grassy footpath between it and the deeply-cut Foulstone Dike, down which you will see the housewife's path winding from the house to the water. On each side of the footpath, grouse batteries have been built. Brogging Moss is on the right, and Foulstone Moor on the left.

The ascent of Derwent Edge by our path is very gradual – a mile in length – but the walk has the true moorland charm, I think, with a growing sense of wildness, remoteness, almost eeriness. You have not risen far before the Wheel Stones (called popularly the Coach and Horses) appear on the ridge to the left front; while the backward view is well worth constantly watching, as Kirk Edge, Ughill, Moscar, and the line of Stanage Edge, are more and more fully displayed. The path, as the top of the moor is neared, usually has stones on either side splashed with white, marking boundaries for shooters.

The little sensation of the gentle ascent is the appearance of the well-named rocks 'Cakes o' Bread' on the left front. Half a dozen steps bring them suddenly into view as if they had risen from the moors. The effect in the evening light, or when mists make things loom large, is strange and rather impressive.

After the Cakes have come into view you soon begin to see over the Edge in front to the right of Dovestone Tor, where Lose Hill, the Edale Back Tor, and Mam Tor are seen as a sharp range almost end on, with the Edale valley to the right. The actual top of the Edge is reached at an upright bridle road stone – Bradfield Gate Head being the name of the spot. At the same time the Derwent Back Tor, which has been bidden during the ascent, appears on the right, a furlong away, the highest of its rocks being crowned with a small cairn.

The height of the Edge where we stand is 1,690 feet. Back Tor is only 75 feet higher. Looking to the left along the ridge of the moor you see a heathery bank raised, and running to where a jutting rock falls precipitously towards the Derwent valley. The bank is the county boundary, and the rock Dovestone Tor. It is the finest plunge of rock on this Edge – finer than you can see from this distance. From the other side of the Derwent valley – say, the Water Board's late rail track – it looks the craggiest height and culminating point of this little moorland range; but Back Tor is a hundred feet higher. You see now why it is called 'Back' Tor. It lies back from the Edge. It is trespass but, although you may be met and turned back, you could walk along the raised county boundary and along the whole of the old shepherds' path along Derwent Edge and have no fear of intruding on a nest.

ON BACK TOR

The wind is always blowing as you sit on the cairn on the topmost slanting rock of Back Tor, and a more empty, homeless scene you cannot find. It is a fitting region for creatures that love loneliness; and you have them near. The curlew calls plaintively across the marshy cloughs. The gun-surviving hawk sails past on easy wing scanning the great hillsides, and the plover wails from the fields that edge the moor below. A hare, startled from amid the rocks, darts off in a straight line, trusting only to

Back Tor, Derwent Edge

its speed, terrified by the unusual sight of man. It is a wild, wide place, far from the ways of men, who here are the most occasional of creatures, and all its notes have the sadness of great spaces – of the mountains, moors, and seas. And yet it does one good to get into this upland, age-long solitude, where the primeval world is felt to be a mighty fact, linked on to us. The spirit of the moors has his throne on Back Tor.

It is worth while to look round and study the district. The Mam Tor range is dwarfed by the long ridge of the Kinderscout Plateau, which from here looks one high continuous level till it is suddenly cut off and drops to the Snake at Fairbrook Naze. That ragged end is the hill of the whole scene. To the right of Kinder there is trenched valley beyond trenched valley up to Bleaklow; and more to the right not only do the confirmatory ridges to the one on which we stand – Howden Edge, Wilfrey Edge, and Margery Hill – stand out clear and high as ourselves, but the scene is backed up by Black Hill (1,908 feet) on the north of Longdendale. Sheffieldward the familiar moorland scenes are spread at our feet.

Along Derwent Edge, in the direction of Ashopton, we see the Cakes o' Bread, quite near at hand, and lying back from the Edge; Dovestone Tor, in front of the 'Cakes', falling to a precipice; and, further along, the curiously thrust up Salt Cellar rock. The Wheel Stones are further off, and more to the left on the moor. In the opposite direction the ridge on which we stand curves to the Lost Lad, traditionally named after a 'lost lad' – a hill with a solitary stone on it. The true line of the moor goes off more to the right, by the Cartledge Stones trench-boundary ridge, and then sweeps back round and above the gullies which sink into Howden Dean, or Chest, and form the finest brook-beginning in this moorland area. The Dean is a huge coombe with a number of small coombes, or cloughs, falling into it all around its head.

WAYS DOWN

If you care for moors you will have enjoyed Back Tor, and will go back to Bradfield Gate Head thankful you have come. But now comes the difficulty of the way down. It may not be distasteful to return the way you came by Foulstone Delf, but there are better ways.

The best way from Back Tor is the 'trespass' way along the county boundary to Dovestone Tor, then along the top to the Salt Cellar – a rock sticking up on the side of the moor; then along the top as near as may be to White Tor, where the pathway runs to the dip between White Tor and Whinstone Lee Tor, where it doubles back to the right and down, and joins a path alongside a wall which, leading past Whinstone Lee Tor, takes you either straight forward to Riding House and Grainfoot farms and Ashopton, or round to the left to Cut-throat Bridge. This is a magnificent walk all the way, with superb views, and no man who ever came this way to see these views would do a pennyworth of harm to the moor or its birds. It is, at present, a trespass walk all along Derwent Edge.

Another way is to follow by the ancient, now contested, bridle road to Derwent, which goes westwards across the bank top of John Field Howden (John Thorpe's field) and by a deep trench on the high side of Mill Brook into the bottom.

The best way to Derwent Chapel for anyone who is not afraid of a short cut away from a path is to take the way described in the last paragraph from Bradfield Gate Head, strike the wall, follow it for some distance, and then drop steeply down by a path and trench track to Ashes Farm and Derwent Chapel. He would be a popular and prized man who restored the public bridle way from Bradfield Gate Head to Derwent Chapel – and along the Edge – for lovers of Nature, whose only reason for rambling is to see the beauty, and feel the elemental charm, of the unspoiled moors.

Nothing keeps alive the spirit of revolt and iconoclasm so fiercely as a refusal to the general community of the use of their eyes over beautiful remote tracts of the earth, under the plea of private ownership. The rocks of twenty thousand years echo laughter at the arrogance of the claim: 'These are mine, and no other men may even pass near and look at them.'

Another well-known explorer of Peakland caves was Sheffield's Francis (Frank) Winder, a past president of the Derbyshire Pennine Club. His main claim to fame was his quirkily titled An Unconventional Guide to the Caverns of Castleton and District, *which was published in 1938 and featured a drawing of an axe-wielding caveman with what appears to be a thoroughly anachronistic dinosaur peering over his shoulder on its cover.*

This is an edited version of Winder's light-hearted description of his first descent of Eldon Hole, one of the fabled Wonders of the Peak, with fellow members of the Derbyshire Pennine Club in 1907.

FRANCIS A. WINDER *An Unconventional Guide to the Caverns of Castleton and District* (1938)

ELDON HOLE

There are few more disagreeable experiences than descending a ladder three hundred feet in length down a shaft which shows indications of collapse, and some of the ancient levels have to be treated with respect.

Eldon Hole is, however, a comparatively harmless place, provided that the gear is sound and has been rigged by competent hands. The method chosen on the occasion now being referred to was a bo'sun's chair attached to the end of a strong and lengthy cable. This, to a novice, appeared sufficiently enthralling, but there were additional complications owing to the chair having to be pulled over the centre of the Hole by another rope.

As the writer was tied into the chair his teeth chattered like castanets, and an attendant slipped something into his mouth. 'Bite on that,' he said, kindly, 'it will stop the noise.' It *did*, for the gag was a tallow candle, and the state of his nerves will be realised when it is mentioned that he did not recognise the taste, and was still chewing the fat with contentment when he arrived at the bottom of the rift.

The dimensions have been given in many books, but to save the reader the trouble of reference, it may be stated that the top of the vertical portion is shaped like a gigantic wedge over a hundred feet in length, and a central width of thirty feet.

The size rapidly decreases, and at a depth of sixty feet from the surface it measures only sixty by fifteen feet. Then it again widens out into a typical cave.

The floor of the chasm, which is really an anteroom to the main chamber, slopes to the south, and is composed of hundreds of tons of

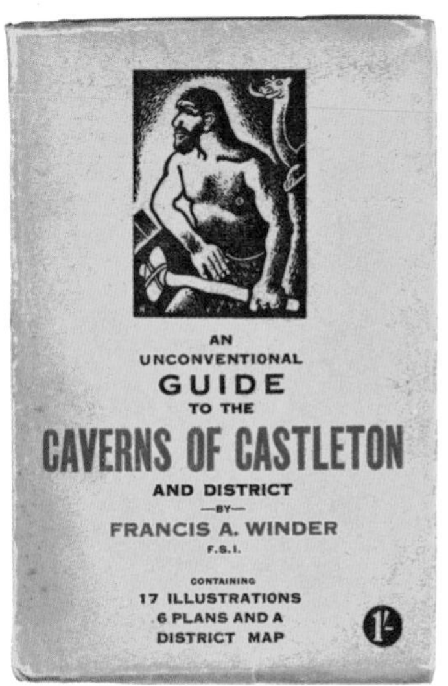

An Unconventional Guide to the Caverns of Castleton and District (1938)

boulders and smaller stones thrown down by tourists in order to hear the noise as the missile rebounds from wall to wall, and finally breaks to pieces on the floor.

It may be mentioned that, at one period, the life of the stone wall which protected the cavity was estimated to be seven years, and annual attention was required to make good the effects of wastage.

A wire fence now surrounds the hole; and, as the strands are useless for sounding purposes the fence has remained intact.

There is a tale told of one absent-minded professor, who wished to estimate the depth by timing the fall of a stone. He took a fragment of rock in one hand, held his gold watch in the other, and then threw the timepiece into the rift. His remarks incidental to the error are known, but cannot well be repeated.

As the writer landed at the point where the watch must have fallen, he heard a yell of warning from above. It was due to the action of an onlooker who had leant against the wall which had collapsed and started a stone avalanche.

Fortunately, the rope was slack, and he rushed for cover with the chair still strapped to his trousers. The incident was useful training for his later experiences in France.

The floor of the outer cavern is formed like a shallow inclined gully, the lower part of which passes through a natural arching in the rock about four feet in height; and, on passing through this portal, he obtained his first view of the main chamber. It appeared very similar in form and size to Lord Mulgrave's Dining-room in the Blue John Cavern, except that the roof was a dome, and the floor sloping and boulder-strewn.

There are still traces of stalagmitic formation on the roof and sides, but these could not be seen, as the interior of the cavern was obscured by smoke from flare-lamps, candles and the ignition of magnesium powder.

On looking round for the remainder of the party he observed Sprules and [J.W.] Puttrell near the right-hand wall, and they were behaving in a similar manner to excited terriers at a rabbit burrow. They had presumably discovered a new passage of which they were endeavouring to open out the entrance.

He was at once pressed into service, and an hour's work cleared the orifice of surplus stones.

It was a typical Derbyshire swallet, waterworn and floored with rounded limestone boulders. They lay at the angle of rest; and, as each stone was removed, two of its adjacent fellows rolled down to take its place.

Then Bishop appeared at the opening, and his mournful face showed that he was having a happy time. He is always that way in a cave.

There were now sufficient workers to form a chain. The boulders were passed from hand to hand, and a way opened for a distance of sixty feet.

Sprules was in the lead, and as he was endeavouring to pick up a particularly elusive pebble, it slipped from his fingers through a chink in the floor. It proceeded downwards with a series of bumps culminating with a squash as it hit some soft resistance.

More stones followed the first one, and then someone suggested that as Sprules was evidently sitting on the top of a hole possessing unknown depth it might be advisable to secure him safely with a rope.

The suggestion was approved, and then a few minutes' work with a crowbar revealed the entrance to a narrow and vertical cleft, evidently a natural swallet.

Sprules, after removing his superfluous apparel, for the route was extremely restricted, forced himself through the chink and wended his way downwards. The writer followed him, steadied by Puttrell from the top with the rope.

The cleft was a delightful place, affording a little rock climb of about thirty feet, just a typical Cumberland gully transferred, as though by a magic wand, into a Derbyshire cave. Even chock-stones were in evidence, wedged between the faces of the living rock.

At the foot of the lowest pitch was a beach of amber-coloured sand, water-washed and evidently blinding the natural overflow of the 'sink'.

Further progress was impossible, as every particle of excavated material would have had to be transported to the higher levels through the eyehole and up the slope of unstable boulders.

This fact was practically demonstrated, for suddenly a kind and learned face looked down from above, and a gentle voice murmured, 'May I too come down?' Simultaneously with the words a rounded stone of the size of a Belisha Beacon shot through the opening, followed by a heavy and nailed boot – the Professor had slipped.

He stuck, but the stone gathered momentum and travelled down the cleft with the velocity of an old-fashioned cannon-ball.

The writer, in a state of absolute terror, watched it fall and counted the number of times it bounced from wall to wall, and as he reached nine a plop indicated that the thunderbolt had landed on the only bit of sand unoccupied by a human form.

The Professor, who was the culprit, was forgiven. He was so gentle and apologetic, and later the writer, for one, was glad he had not been unkind. The strain of the descent and the long walk back to Castleton proved too much for the old man's feeble frame, and brought on an illness which proved to be a prelude to his decease.

The incident of the stone was the last excitement of the evening; and a couple of hours later every member of the party had regained the surface, tired in body but contented in mind.

Whether further discoveries of importance will be made with reference to the cavern it is hard to say. There appears to be little doubt that there is some relation between Eldon Hole and the Castleton caves, but whether such a communication will ever be established is a matter of conjecture. The writer is, however, informed that a party of explorers, not connected with the Pennine Club, have made progress below the level of the sandy beach.

If a through route could be established with either the Speedwell Cavern or the Peak, the achievement would rank as one of the most important in the history of the district; but it is hoped that the clothes of the explorers will not be burnt from off their backs like the feathers of the goose which came in contact with the purgatorial fires.

The following is a rather grudging opinion of the Peak from The Untutored Townsman's Invasion of the Countryside, *written in 1946 by Professor C.E.M. Joad, a regular on the popular Home Service radio programme* The Brains Trust, *and an ardent campaigner for the right of public access to mountain and moor. He wrote it after he had addressed an access rally in The Winnats Pass, Castleton, during which he had controversially told ramblers, 'if you want the moors to be free, you must free them for yourselves', which many saw as an invitation to trespass, an assumption which Joad later somewhat controversially denied.*

C.E.M. JOAD *The Untutored Townsman's Invasion of the Countryside* (1946)

I am not an enthusiast for the Peak District. It is wild; it is even grand, but the grandeur partakes of the savage rather than of the beautiful. All the ingredients which make the north of England so attractive to the southerner are present; hills and rocks, heather-clad moorlands, swift rushing streams of clear water, wide views; above all, the sense of space and remoteness. For this is a big country; it is austere, almost scornful in its disdain for the adventitious prettinesses of flower and coppice and hedgerow. It can be formidable, too; to be lost in a mist on Kinder Scout and put to the necessity of dropping into and climbing out of the deep peat ditches with which the top of that gloomy plateau is seamed and scarred is no joke, while the outcropping rocks of blackened gritstone, grim enough at all times, when the mist comes down and the rain falls look very forbidding indeed . . . Perhaps because I like the adventitious prettiness, like at least to know that it is not too far off and is there for the visiting when I want it, I have never taken this country to my heart as I have the Lakes . . .

In all this I am, it is clear, speaking only for myself and I bid myself beware of the temptation to treat my private tastes and fancies, dictated by who knows what accidental associations, into canons of aesthetic judgment. Also I am speaking only of the northern area of what is called the Peak District. I have said nothing of the green and friendlier country which stretches on the south nearly to Bakewell; of Hope Valley and Cave Dale, of Bretton Clough and Middleton Dale, of Miller's Dale and Monsal Dale, of Grindleford and the valley of the Derwent. There are high moors between these Dales, but the greenness, the curving contours and the wide views to the high escarpments which lie on their boundaries, Axe Edge to the west, Curbar, Baslow and Stanage to the

In Grindsbrook Clough, Kinder Scout

east and Rushup and Grindsbrook to the north, give an impression of grandeur without unfriendliness. Here week-end after week-end come men and women from Sheffield and Derby, from the Derbyshire coalfields and the Staffordshire potteries.

But the Manchester men with whom I have chiefly gone in company make for the grimmer country to the north, which evokes an affection amounting at times to a fanatical zeal as weekend after week-end they tramp vast distances over the moors.

And how well they know it! To go with one of them over Bleaklow or the Stanage Moors is to tap a knowledge of the countryside which only a great personal love could have inspired. How, too, they champion it against the Lakes, against the Dales, against even Scotland itself.

Perhaps they champion it the more eagerly for the disability under which it and they labour, for upon all this country lies a curse, the curse of the keeper.

CROCODILE IN THE PEAK

I shall not easily forget the first time I saw the curse in operation. I had gone out from Manchester early on a Sunday morning in April for my first view of the Peak District. I found the Central Station alive with ramblers, all dressed up for a day's walk on the Derbyshire moors, complete with rucksacks, hobnail boots and shorts.

My walk started from Hayfield and we found ourselves almost at once on a path leading on to the moor. It was a gorgeous path commanding wide views over miles of moorland country and finally descending steeply by Jacob's Ladder to Edale. It was, of course, unfenced and on either side of it there stretched for mile upon mile the empty spaces of the moor. The walk, nevertheless, was a disappointment, for we were not unaccompanied. Straggling along the path both in front and behind there must have been hundreds of walkers; indeed, so close were we packed that we looked for all the world like a girls' school taking the air in 'crocodile' on a Sunday afternoon.

Why did we keep so religiously to the path as though we were ants on a run? Because to leave it was to brave an encounter with the keepers, and being for the most part law-abiding folk, we were prepared to be penned, cribbed, cabined, and confined rather than transgress the rights of private property. Yet so confined, we were deprived of the healing power of solitude, deprived of the exhilaration of emptiness and vastness, deprived of the sense of spaciousness which are the great gifts of the moors by which we were surrounded, but which we were denied.

In this whole area of uncultivated moorland which lies between Manchester and Sheffield, an area of over 230 square miles, there are only twelve public footpaths which are more than two miles long; of the 150,000-odd acres involved, only 1,212 acres are open to the public; 109,000 acres are in private ownership, while 39,000 are owned by Local Authorities who mysteriously debar the citizens whom they are supposed to represent from access to the land of which they as citizens are part owners. The Peak itself, a bare plateau of some thirteen square miles, is uncrossed by a single right of way. Bleaklow, thirty-seven square miles in extent, which is only sixteen miles from Manchester and sixteen from Sheffield, boasts not a single footpath. For Bleaklow, in common with most of the rest of this country, is preserved for the shooting of grouse. Upon it, the hand of the keeper lies heavy; walkers are frowned at by notice boards and everywhere trespassers are prosecuted. Hence to leave the path was to risk an encounter with a keeper, with the certainty of being cursed and the possibility of being prosecuted. Let us see what it means to encounter a keeper.

ENCOUNTERS WITH A KEEPER

I am with a party – it is, in fact, a club – of ramblers from Manchester and we are ascending Kinder Scout by Kinder Downfall, where a fairly substantial stream makes its way in a series of leaps down a gorge. It is a hot day in June and, as the party includes several inexperienced walkers, it takes us a couple of hours to reach the top. We sit down and rest; we are, in point of fact, having our lunch and enjoying the view which to the north extends over many miles of moorland, when we hear ourselves hailed by a voice. We turn round and see a man approaching with gun, stick, dog and threatening aspect.

'Off with you,' he says. 'You know you are not allowed here.'

I am for expostulating; for explaining that we are doing no damage, that we are peaceable and ordinary citizens who have left the prison of the towns in order to enjoy the air of the countryside and to look at the view, that we have only just finished fighting – this, by the way, was in 1920 – to preserve, or so we had been told, the freedom of the land of our forefathers, and that as free men we are jolly well going to enjoy it and that he ought to be ashamed of himself – hired lackey of the rich, that he is – for trying to stop us, and so on with more to the same effect. In case my eloquence and arguments produced no result – I don't suppose for a moment they would have had any – I should have led the keeper a dance (I could run in those days) in and out of the ditches which criss-cross the top of Kinder Scout.

However, I was not the leader of the party and the leader said none of these things. He was a docile chap – most ramblers, by the way, are; they come from the class that has for centuries been used to obeying rather than to issuing orders – and all he said was, 'But we have only just got up to the top of Kinder and the ladies are tired and want to rest. Can't we, please, stay for another ten minutes before we go down again?' This had no effect. We must get up, the keeper said, and get off at once. If we did not, he would find means to make us and, as if to make good his word, he marched forward and stood over us, threatening us until such time as we had hurriedly put together the remains of our lunch, after which with our tails between our legs we allowed ourselves to be hustled off the plateau, the keeper, still complete with dog, stick and gun, shepherding us until we were well down into the valley.

Earlier in the same book, Joad also described the boom in rambling which followed the Second World War, and the scene at Manchester's Central Station at weekends.

You can see living witness of this revolution at the Central Station in Manchester early on a Sunday morning, complete with rucksacks, shorts and hob-nailed boots, waiting for the early trains to Edale, Hope and the Derbyshire moors. Looking at them, one might be tempted to think that the whole of Manchester was in exodus; justifiably, since these northern cities are by any reckoning the ugliest conglomeration of bricks and mortar with which mankind has ever defaced the unprotesting surface of the earth. For over a hundred years men and women stayed in these places because they must, worked in them, played in them and on Sundays, when piety forbade games, lounged in their streets and waited for the pubs to open. In our day, hiking has replaced beer as the shortest cut out of Manchester, as turning their backs upon the cities which their fathers made, armies of young people make sorties at any and every opportunity into the countryside.

The classic book on the history of walking and climbing in the Peak is Eric Byne and Geoffrey Sutton's 1966 masterpiece High Peak. *Though now sadly both out of date and out of print,* High Peak *is still the bible for those wanting to know how and why the Peak became such a Mecca for walking and climbing. It is especially strong on the early days of rock climbing, when working class climbers such as Joe Brown and Don Whillans from Manchester took the sport to new levels of difficulty on the crags of Stanage Edge and The Roaches.*

Byne, a Birmingham man who had climbed with many of the early pioneers, was the editor of Rock Climbs in the Peak, *while Sutton was a climber, biographer and poet who for some years was principal of Derbyshire County Council's White Hall Centre for Outdoor Pursuits near Buxton. This excerpt is from the introduction.*

ERIC BYNE and GEOFFREY SUTTON *High Peak: The Story of Walking and Climbing in the Peak District* (1966)

Schoolchildren in the south of England are taught that somewhere north of Derby there is a mountain called The Peak which is the highest in the southern Pennines. Maps frequently foster the illusion. One of the authors was brought up in this belief, and it was like learning the truth about Santa Claus all over again to find that he would never be able to climb this mountain – though he has since met persons who claimed to have done so. In fact, as everybody in the north of England knows, the district takes its name not from any mountain or proliferation of mountains but from the name of a tribe that once inhabited it. From their language come many familiar names: *Cyn dwr scwd*, the hill of the waterfall, has become our Kinder Scout; *dwr gwent*, the white water, is the Derwent; and the many 'lows', Kinderlow, Bleaklow, Shuttlings Low and all the others, indicate burial places. Whether all these were indeed tombs or whether the similarity between a tumulus and a hill gave rise to these names is a matter for investigation. The habit of naming mountains thus is far-flung. In Welsh the name for Snowdon is y Wyddfa, the tomb; and there is also the Alpine Tombe Murée. That mountaintops were thought fit graves for kings is no wonder. Our early forebears seem to have had a taste for the highest and most uncomfortable places, perhaps because the undrained valleys were full of tangled woods. It must have been cold crouching behind the walls of Carl Wark or Mam Tor, or curling up to sleep on skins by a fire on the floor of Thor's Cave. Did they go visiting each other from the settlement behind Gardom's Edge to what later became Robin Hood's Cave? Did bands of them climb Kinder to worship, at a set season, over the altar that was found near Ringing Roger? Were the same rites observed in the deep cleft of Ludchurch? We have only a few broken pots and mysterious stone circles, such as the famous ones at Arbor Low and around Cork Stone, to remind us that the tracks we follow over the highest ground were not all worn by modern feet, and that eyes we cannot guess at must have kindled with pleasure at the same views we now briefly enjoy. These hills have always drawn men of independent mind. William Peveril, bastard son of the Conqueror, lorded it from Castleton, but needed his gaunt tower for his continuance. More legendary Robin Hood lived out his four-score years of freedom here, in defiance of authority. Later, in the reign of Henry V, the Lollards held their forbidden conventicles in the winding chasm of Ludchurch, supposedly named after one of them, where later Squire Trafford of Swythamley leapt his horse fifteen feet over the gap, which is sixty feet deep. Later still Charlotte and Emily Brontë were inspired by the remoteness of these moors, for *Jane Eyre* is staged at Hathersage, and *Wuthering Heights,* a little away to the north, might be anywhere here. George Eliot wrote of the country around Ashbourne as 'Stonyshire' and Mrs Humphrey Ward wrote parts of her *History of David Grieve* at Upper House under Kinder. Edward Carpenter, a founder of socialism, lived near Grindleford – and the list goes on of minds rooted in the freedom of the windswept moorlands. Perhaps it is not a coincidence that the wind is in so many of the names: Windgate Edge, Winnats, Windgather, Windyharbour – and you can hear it in Ringing Roger, Coldspring, Wild Moor, Gathering Hill, Starkholmes, and Within Lache.

Geologically the Peak is divided into two, sometimes known as the Dark and the White Peak. The Dark, which is of millstone grit, extends in a horseshoe around the limestone of the White Peak and stretches away to the north. It is mostly high ground, consisting of moorland peat-plateaux stretching into seemingly immeasurable distances, much of it close to 2,000 feet, reaching 2,088 feet around Crowden Head on Kinder Scout. Even the valleys are high and desolate, with swift-running streams. The soil is sour and the climate, for Britain, harsh. Agriculture is difficult and trees are rare. In historical times there were herds of wild ponies and packs of wolves. Red deer were once so plentiful that they are said to have trampled men and dogs, but they are now confined to a few parks such as Chatsworth – a number of them met a prosaic but useful end in the soup kitchens of big cities during the depression.

Ringing Roger, Kinder Scout

Nowadays the wildest beasts are perhaps the arctic hares that inhabit the tops of Kinder and Bleaklow (usually remaining brown in the snow and turning white just as it melts: they were introduced artificially from Scandinavia) and the foxes that hunt them; but the very spirit of such places seems concentrated in the cries of the curlew and grouse which make them their homes. It is a land of deserted level distances and isolated sheep-farms except where dingy mill and market towns straggle along the deeper valleys. Even the fleece of the sheep is dark with the grime from Manchester and Sheffield that descends out of the air. The farms look sturdy and embattled against the weather. The bare table-lands make you realise the sky as you never do in more closed country.

By contrast the white drystone walls and green fields of the White Peak seem almost soft. But this dry rolling country is also subject to quarrying, the curse of all limestone country in Britain, and since the rock is particularly rich in calcium in this area it is much sought industrially. The valleys of the White Peak, especially the important Derwent valley, are lower than those of the Dark. Agriculture is much less specialised than in the gritstone areas; crops are grown, and there are many cattle. Because of the water difficulty the round dew-ponds are a common sight. But whereas the glory of the Dark Peak is its hilltops, that of the limestone country is in the dales. Usually narrow and not to be guessed at from a short distance away, they wind with their clear streams among woods and gorges and grassy banks of continually changing beauty. There are many beautiful scenes in Britain, but in their own way the Derbyshire dales are unrivalled.

Sheffield singer songwriter Sally Goldsmith wrote this song on the occasion of the sixtieth anniversary of the Mass Trespass in 1992. She says she wanted to make a link between all those varied people who find recreation on moor and mountain today and all those unremitting campaigners who made it possible. Although the song is called 'Trespassers Will Be Celebrated', she tried to acknowledge all those who played their part, from negotiators to proponents of direct action. She also wanted this lovely image of land campaigners over history taking a walk together – hoping that Benny Rothman would have been pleased to be walking with Wat Tyler!

SALLY GOLDSMITH 'Trespassers Will Be Celebrated' (1992)

Joan alone on Stanage
Finds the air to clear her head
Lift her spirits, calm her nerves and bring her peace
While the ramblers group is raring
To walk Bleaklow's boggy wastes
Kitted out with compass, map and fleece

Hassan's on his first trip with his classmates from his school
He's never heard the eerie curlew cry
All owe their Sunday freedom to those who went before
The ones who tried to reach out for the sky

Trespassers will be celebrated
Now their will is done
Trespassers will be celebrated
Glorious kingdom come
By those who walk the southern downs,
The high and windy moor
Trespassers will be celebrated
Freedom is won

Gill and Tony's little family
Clamber madly over stones
Delight in rushing streams and frightened sheep
The baby's in her backpack
Rocking gently through her dreams
And cooing with the beck from deep in sleep
Rose and Madge are wandering, their working life is done
Their time's their own, they range for miles around
While blokes out on the Roaches crawl like spiders up the rock
But know nought of those who won this hallowed ground [Chorus]

See campaigners through the ages
Walk together side by side
Wat Tyler, Benny Rothman hand-in-hand
Carpenter, Winstanley and the Diggers on the hill
The commoners who dared to seize the land

Stephen Morton, Barbara Castle,
Bert Ward and Terry Howard
The Greenham women cutting down the fence
Elsie Gaskell and the Buntings, young Woodcraft singers too,
Tom Stephenson, MacColl and Thomas Spence [Chorus]

Remember those who stuck at nothing
But kept slogging up the hill
For the right to spread their wings and take their space
Negotiators, demonstrators, all who spun the dream
That you and me might claim our rightful place
Trespassed for us and against those
Who kept beauty for themselves
Who fenced us out for profit and for greed
But now the way is open for us all to share this land
And the beauty and the glory's ours indeed [Chorus]

G.H.B ('Bert') Ward (centre, in white jumper) trespassing with fellow Clarion Ramblers on Kinder Scout in January 1924 (from Days of Sunshine and Rain by Ann Beedham, 2011).

6.
MODERN WRITERS

Because of its situation so close to the teeming cities of Manchester, Sheffield and the Midlands, the Peak has long been the playground for walkers and climbers. Among them have been some of the finest modern outdoor writers, such as Patrick Monkhouse, John Hillaby, Roger Redfern and Jim Perrin.

Roger Redfern had for many years been the doyen of Peak District outdoor writers before his untimely death in 2011. Born and brought up on the eastern outskirts of the Peak near Chesterfield, he wrote about the area for fifty years, and produced many well-researched and knowledgeable articles. He had been a Guardian *Country Diarist for many years, and the following is a excerpt from his first book.*

ROGER REDFERN *Rambles in Peakland* (1965)

Of all the limestone hills known to me the most beautiful trio are Chrome Hill, Parkhouse Hill and Thorpe Cloud. They overlook the River Dove on its true left bank, the first two not far below its source, the third fifteen miles farther downstream.

Chrome and Parkhouse form a small range, together with Hollins Hill to the north-west and Hitter Hill, Aldery Cliff and High Wheeldon to the south-east. Earl Sterndale, about 4½ miles south of Buxton, is the nearest village to this group of hills. I consider the best views of Chrome and Parkhouse to be from the steep slopes immediately eastward of the village while Chrome presents a most dramatic silhouette when seen from the crest of Axe Edge, three miles to the north-west.

Parkhouse Hill

Thorpe Cloud

Both hills appear far bigger and higher than they are, a distortion due to a combination of their sharp shapes and isolated position above the Dove. They are superb examples of fossiliferous limestone reefs projecting through the surrounding shales. It is not hard to believe that they were formed by the accumulation of fossils in a warm sea long ago, before the younger grits and shales were deposited by river estuaries. These more recent deposits eventually covered the reefs. For unknown ages the superlative forms lay in the darkness under the newer rocks. Only the subsequent action of weathering has removed this latter material to reveal the reefs again. Continued activity on the part of frost, rain, wind and sun has dramatised their profiles – a process which is still going on. It is an interesting exercise to imagine what these twin hills will look like in another five thousand years!

From Earl Sterndale Church walk down to the inn and turn right towards the main Buxton–Longnor road and turn left down towards Longnor for a quarter of a mile to Glutton Farm. We are virtually at the foot of the east ridge of Parkhouse Hill here and it is a simple matter to walk up the steep, scrub-dotted slope to the sharp, white crest. Chrome Hill appears near to the west, and the smooth slopes of the upper Dove valley lie below, to the south. We are little more than 1,000 feet above sea level. Drop down the steep and stony west ridge into Dowel Dale.

Farther up this limestone dale are numerous caves where prehistoric man lived and his remains are now giving scope to the archaeologist's explorations. Continuing slightly north of west we are quickly upon Chrome's east ridge and when the top is reached we are just over 1,200 feet above sea level. Among the broken reef rocks of Chrome is a cavern called the Devil's House and Parlour. An old tradition states that the Devil came here to hang himself but didn't manage it, so he haunts the hill-top daily from midnight to dawn.

The 1,274-foot high Hollins Hill rises to the north-west but this is not so beautiful of shape, though a burial mound on the summit is an object of encouragement to climb.

From the top of both Chrome Hill and Parkhouse Hill the western horizon is shadowed by the graceful gritstone eminences of the West Moor – Morridge, Oliver Hill and Axe Edge. If you decide to walk that way one of the best routes is to cross the Dove to Hollinsclough hamlet. Less than a mile to the south-east of this place, by the lane to Longnor, is Moss Carr. This is a peat bog boasting a very rich flora. If time allows one should go there, especially in late spring or summer. In this low, wet area the bogbean (*Menyanthes trifoliata*) still flourishes, as does marsh cinquefoil (*Potentilla palustris*), spotted orchid (*Dactylorchis maculata* subsp. *ericetorum*) and the recently located dwarf purple orchid (*Orchis pur-purella*).

This is, of course, one of the major attractions of the limestone country as far as I am concerned. The flora of the Carboniferous limestone of the Peak District is very varied and in early summer especially one can spend many happy hours discovering a host of flowering species in the delicate colouring of the deeper dales and on the hill slopes.

Then up the steep lane from Moss Carr for almost three miles beyond Hollinsclough to the Leek–Buxton road (A53) close to Flash Head. Just down to the left (south) before the main road is reached is a damp hollow. In this the River Manifold is born, in this district called Flash Head.

Continuing northwards along the main road for half a mile a farmhouse is reached, standing on the left-hand side of the road. Over the front door is carved 'Dove Head' and if you look down the field on the right-hand side of the road (just opposite the farmhouse) you will notice a stone-flagged path leading diagonally to the corner of the field. Take this clean and well-set slabbed path which leads to a spring in a few yards. This is the source of the world-famous River Dove, or so most people agree. There are a few who don't, and would assign the source to a rushy moor-stream which rises near the top of Axe Edge a mile to the north, but tradition firmly asserts this to be the source.

Now look at the slab on the top of the stone trough. On it are carved the interlocking initials of Izaak Walton and Charles Cotton. These notable angling partners are said to have followed their beloved river to its source and on finding the Springs of Dove carved their initials on the slab over the source. However, the carving is only 110 years old and as Walton died in 1683 and Cotton in 1687 the story cannot be true; in fact, a skilled stone-mason executed the carving, with more than a touch of romanticism. In 1903 the stone was cracked by a hard frost but this has not spoilt the actual initials.

A little to the north of Dove Head the road can be left and Axe Edge ascended. The first top is just over 1,800 feet above sea level and a mile of northward walking over tussock grass brings us to the 1,810 foot top of the edge. There is a triangulation station here and on a clear day the views are extensive.

Eight hundred feet below to the north-east is Buxton with the great bulk of Combs Moss and distant Ladder Hill behind; and behind Combs Moss the mass of Kinder Scout leads to the hills of the north. Round the western horizon as the eye swings are Shining Tor – 24 feet higher than our viewpoint –the Cat and Fiddle, the summit of Shutlingsloe looking very big, and the dip slope of the Roaches. To the south-east are the green and swelling vales of the Manifold and the Dove, then smooth Hollins Hill and Chrome Hill – looking for all the world like a miniature Pumori. Away to the east the tree-topped ridges of the limestone land fade into vagueness.

The River Dove forms the border between Derbyshire and Staffordshire for its entire length from Dove Head to its confluence with the Trent near Burton-upon-Trent (with a few slight deviations southwards from Rocester). Thirteen and a half miles downstream from Chrome and Parkhouse that third notable limestone hill comes into view round a deeply-wooded bend in Dovedale.

Thorpe Cloud, too, is a reef knoll, a prominent monument to the Carboniferous age, having weathered less rapidly than the surrounding limestone. It is lower than the former pair, its top being only 942 feet above sea level; though it is not less imposing for this.

From the village of Thorpe the Cloud is easily climbed. Upon reaching the top you will at once see what a commanding position it holds as a sentinel to Dovedale's southern mouth. It really forms the eastern gatepost to the Dale – Bunster Hill forms the western gatepost. The Dale appears directly below as you peer from the white crest. The Cloud's most noble profile is seen from the vicinity of the Peveril of the Peak Hotel, and the last time I ascended the hill was from this hotel, at sunset on an August evening in company with a friend.

On the top the last light vanished beyond the gritstone West Moor, somewhere beyond the Roaches. Suddenly far below lights flickered through unseen trees; a car was heading away from the mouth of Dovedale 500 feet directly underneath our feet. The sheep were our only companions in the warm night.

The following is Redfern's last Guardian *Country Diary, published a few days after his death in November, 2011. Interestingly, he uses the antique word 'belvedere', often employed by his great hero, the great landscape photographer Walter Poucher (1891-1988), to describe a viewpoint.*

ALDERLEY EDGE

It could have been A.E. Housman all over again! The woods were certainly in trouble as we gained the crest of the ruddy sandstone escarpment atop this dramatic Cheshire belvedere. We leaned against the gale as we looked north-east from Castle Rock towards the western ramparts of Peakland; dark clouds whipped out of Wales bringing grey ladders of downpours. Then the sun shone briefly through the edge-top trees as we strode on otwards the Armada Beacon. Prehistoric inhabitants came here to harvest coloured clays and in the Bronze Age the beacon was used as a burial mound. In 1588 it was chosen as a spot to light signal fires if the Spanish had invaded. Those moaning woods we trod the other day did not exist before the late eighteenth century – the Edge was described as 'a dreary common'. Then the Stanleys of Nether Alderley planted mainly Scots pine on the higher parts, so now we have the bonus of delightful woods hanging on the steep north-eastern flanks and right along the top – woods that also contain Spanish chestnut that now adds autumn gold to complement the last yellow leaves of silver birch.

Heading south, we reached the area mined from the Bronze Age for its abundant copper ore. It was mining that continued into the twentieth century and, later, gave territory for amateur adventurers. Joe Brown and his pals began their climbing careers here, exploring the dangerous shafts and tunnels, and, of course, Alan Garner set some of his magical stories here. The Victorian and earlier plantings transformed a bleak upland ridge into a shining playground that now belongs to the National Trust and at this time of year [November] becomes a multi-coloured fairyland; we traversed the ridge-top, avoiding the worst of those westerlies, but were still able to espy the advancing rainbows through gaps in the trees.

When Leeds-born John Hillaby died in 1996, one obituary described him as 'the most celebrated pedestrian in England'. And when his Journey through Britain *was published in 1968, it was described by one reviewer as 'a classic in travel literature . . . as exciting as any trip through the Amazon jungle'. It has remained a classic of walking literature because it was written by a walker who had a journalist's eye for a story, and a naturalist's eye for detail. His description of the barren summit of Kinder Scout has seldom been bettered.*

JOHN HILLABY *Journey through Britain* (1968)

Kinder that week-end looked pretty good, but walkers came back daubed with greasy-brown dirt. 'What's it like up there?' I asked them. 'A push-over,' said the warden. 'Nothing to it.'

'Dreadful,' said a scraggy little schoolteacher from Leeds. 'All right on the way down,' added his friend, enigmatically. 'Don't try it,' advised somebody else. 'Squishy,' they told me. 'Don't get bogged down on the official caper. Head for the Snake Road on a compass bearing. Kinder's just a load of crap.' Aside from the warden's enthusiasm, opinions ranged from the stoical to downright depressing.

But what *was* it like? Thinking about those opinions now, I recall something that Jack Dempsey, the prize-fighter, is reputed to have said years ago.

During his bouts with Gene Tunney for the heavyweight championship of the world, the Press built up the image of Tunney as the athletic intellectual. They wrote about his reading, his prodigious memory and so on. By contrast, Dempsey seemed to be a dim-wit. But one reporter recalled seeing some books in his dressing-room. One of them was Jeffery Farnol's *Gentleman Jim,* the story of the prize-ring. He asked the prize-fighter what he thought of the book.

Snowy dusk on Kinder

Dempsey, the inarticulate, shook his head, slowly, fumbling for words. 'It wasn't like that,' he said. 'It wasn't like that at all.'

Kinder and Bleaklow are only little hills. You can get over both of them in half a day. But they weren't like what I had been told. They weren't like that at all.

To get up onto the crest you follow a stream that gushes down the narrow V-shaped valley. It is, in fact, more of a corrie than a valley. It gets progressively steeper and then tails off into a cleft that ends in a natural staircase of millstone grit.

The weather that morning looked uncomfortable: misty, with rather nasty-looking clouds. 'It'll hold,' said the warden. And hold it did, just. The path beside the stream had been churned up like a football field by the pedestrian traffic of the previous two days, but there wasn't a bit of rubbish, not so much as an empty cigarette packet, to be seen. They are tidy folk, those northern walkers.

But where had they got to, those people who had swarmed into Edale? They had apparently all gone home. They were out for the day. In the eleven days it took me to get from Edale to the Border I saw in all only about seven or eight walkers.

Up the staircase I went, climbing rapidly, the supercharger undampened by the mist that got worse the higher I got. There is nothing particularly arduous about that spectacular cleft. The feet fall naturally on the dull gritstone boulders rolled down by the floods. They lie one above the other. The surprise is at the top.

Up there you blink. A silent and utterly sodden world. This, surely, is not the summit of the High Peak. Mounds of bare peat rise in all directions, like waves, or rather a field furrowed by a gigantic plough. On the top there are no signposts, no markers. Only the choice of channels between the chocolate-coloured peat.

I took a compass fix on the highest point I could recognize, Crowden

Head, drew a little cross on the map and hurried along the almost dry bed of a stream. There are several of these drainage channels. Too many. The one I followed swung off in the wrong direction. I tried another with the same result. *And* another until, fed-up with the sight of peat, I took off my shoes and socks and climbed on to a crest of the soggy stuff. I didn't sink in far, but the prospect from the top was appalling. The peat extended for miles. It rose, gradually, in the direction of a mound of rocks. And it steamed, like manure. Manure is the analogy that comes most readily to mind. The top of Kinder Scout looks as if it's entirely covered in the droppings of dinosaurs.

To get to the top of the waterfall that leaps off the ledge below Kinder I walked bare-footed, steering by compass which is a laborious business. The trick is to sound the depth of the peat. The light, the almost biscuit-coloured patches are infinitely more bearable than the chocolate-coloured stuff, which is usually wet and deep. It depends on how wet it is. The directions given in the pamphlet are unhelpful. They relate to the names of streams which all look much alike.

From the summit of Kinder, the official route takes you through at least two impressive bogs between Mill Hill and Featherbed Moss, just above the road called the Snake that dissects the moors. I cannot understand this Spartan predilection for what seems to be the longest and most arduous distance between fixed points. Perhaps the terrain has changed since the route was last surveyed, officially. There are people, I know, who speak highly of these south Pennine moors. They like the atmosphere of wilderness. I am not among them. I found them extraordinarily depressing.

From the botanical point of view, they are examples of land at the end of its tether. All the life has been drained off or burnt out, leaving behind only the acid peat. You can find nothing like them anywhere else in Europe. Here is the end-product of what botanists call a succession. The ancient woodlands that flourished after the ice melted degenerated into boggy patches of land, wet certainly, but rich in flowers. But as a result of burning, tree felling and overgrazing the land became progressively more sour. It lost its capacity to sustain more than a handful of plants, such as the bilberry, the mosses and the liverworts. On the summit of Kinder even the bilberry has gone. The heavily-dissected peat is bare. The faint cheep of pipits sounds like the last ticks of a clock that has almost run down.

Looking down on the Snake Road I saw what from that height appeared to be a beetle lying on its back, surrounded by ant-like figures. A car had crashed and turned over. A model for which it is claimed that all the parts are replaceable had skidded, hit a rock and disintegrated. The driver, fortunately, had been thrown clear before it overturned, but the car had come to pieces.

You cross the road and climb up to another pike of shapeless rocks called Bleaklow Head, where the scenery is very much like Kinder. Perhaps a bit more depressing, for here and there are sheep and the sheep are filthy.

Towards mid-afternoon the mist thickened. With uneasy memories of Dartmoor, I hastened on, guided for the most part by the pencil-thin mast of Holme Moss television station. It lies due north. The pamphlet says: head due north. This is an error or, at best, a loose statement, since it leads you into a difficult defile called Wildboar Clough. I got in and, with difficulty, I got out. I didn't really mind, for the Kinder caper was nearly over and I don't suppose I shall ever go there again.

That night the couple in charge of the Youth Hostel at Crowden treated me with such warmth that I couldn't say anything about my dislike of the moors around them, and in the morning, of course, I felt much better.

Hannah Mitchell, born and brought up on the remote Alport Castles Farm in the shadow of Bleaklow, ran away from home after a mere fortnight's schooling, which had involved a daily walk across the moors to Glossop. Freed from the constrictions of an unloving mother and farm life, Hannah became a radical suffragist and member of the Independent Labour Party, speaking on platforms with the Pankhursts. She later became a Manchester city councillor and magistrate.

This is Hannah's account of the two events which were welcome highlights in a generally miserable childhood, taken from her 1968 autobiography, The Hard Way Up. *The famous annual Methodist celebration, the Alport Castles Lovefeast, was held on the family farm, and the Hiring Fair at Hope six miles away in the Hope Valley.*

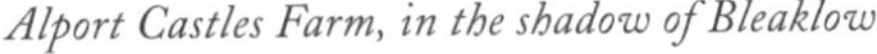

Alport Castles Farm, in the shadow of Bleaklow

HANNAH MITCHELL *The Hard Way Up* (1968)

There were two red-letter days in the year which I love to recall. Chief among them was the annual Love-feast, an ancient religious festival held in high summer in my father's barn. This event was much thought of in the neighbourhood and indeed in many places much further afield.

Weeks beforehand my mother spring-cleaned, papered and white-washed, we girls scrubbed and polished inside the house, while the boys painted the window frames and the house doors green. All the farm buildings were whitewashed inside, the doors painted a clean stone colour. The yard was swept, the gardens weeded, even the big stone water-trough was emptied and scrubbed, until when refilled it sparkled as if set with diamonds.

On the day preceding the event, the big barn was emptied and swept, the floor strewn with rushes and bracken, rough planks supported by big stones arranged as seats; a trestle table served as a platform, the big Bible and hymn books from the Chapel were brought in, and all was ready.

My mother baked bread, pies and cakes, roasted a great piece of beef, and boiled a ham, while we got out the best china and table-linen and set tables in the parlour, or 'house-place', and in the big kitchen. On Sunday morning we rose early, for by nine o'clock the worshippers began to arrive, mostly on foot, as the big coaches from the distant towns had to be left at the end of the narrrow lane. Groups of twenty or thirty arriving in this isolated spot seemed a multitude to us, who rarely saw a stranger from one year's end to another.

Most of the visitors had left home so early they needed breakfast on their arrival, so all morning we were busy serving great pots of tea and jugs of milk and preparing the cold lunch, which was offered to all our friends and relatives.

At one o'clock the Lovefeast began with the singing of a hymn, 'Jesu lover of my soul' being the favourite, and prayer followed by the breaking of bread. Baskets filled with substantial slices of cake were handed round by the stewards. Each person took a portion and a draught of water from the vessels offered, then the meeting was open for all to bear testimony to the faith they professed. Old revival hymns, and half-forgotten choruses were recalled and sung with fervour; simple testimonies were offered and heartfelt prayers couched in homely language ascended to the throne of grace.

I always felt that some unusual story was attached to this yearly Pentecost, but it was many years before I found out that this place was linked by association with the persecution of the Covenanters under the 'Act of Uniformity' in 1662. At this remote spot men and women assembled to worship God in their own way, and, one hopes, were never discovered by their enemies. Tradition has it that John Wesley himself had preached in the barn, so it seemed a natural supposition that the founders of the Wesleyan Society should choose this spot, already consecrated by those early worshippers, for their annual festival, and to it we all return, making our yearly visit like pilgrims returning to a shrine.

Another event was the hiring-fair at Hope six miles away, which we were allowed to attend. This village has always been my 'Land of heart's desire', an old-world, green, little spot greyed over with the dust of many centuries. Standing in the churchyard facing the single street, fringed with small stone houses and gay little gardens, all facing the church, I always experienced a feeling of peace and rest as one who came home after long absence. My sensations here, even as a child, have strengthened my belief in reincarnation. I did not know then, as I learned later, that this place was the cradle of my race, that the stone coffin lids in the church had covered the graves of my ancestors who had held high office in the land centuries before.

'Simple faith' may indeed be more than Norman blood, but few of us are not thrilled by the knowledge that our family tree had its roots deep in the soil of our lovely country.

The fair at Hope was the time from which all contracts for service were dated and early in the day youths and maidens wishing to 'better themselves' by a change of situation gathered in the village, grouping themselves by the churchyard railings to be interviewed by prospective employers who, after some preliminary bargaining about wages, would hand over the 'fastening penny', usually a florin, and after mutual agreements as to the date of entering service, it being the custom to take a few days' holiday at this time, all were free to enjoy themselves.

First the dinner of roast beef and plum pudding, which all the inns provided on fair day. Next we sampled the various entertainments, bought nuts, gingerbread and 'fairings' from the stalls which lined the streets. These were usually shawls, handkerchiefs, beads and brooches. Then games and dancing on the village green till twilight fell. For lovers the walk home in the scented darkness crowned the day's delights.

These two events were the highlights in an otherwise dull life made needlessly unhappy by my mother's temper, which seemed to grow worse, so that we all sought early release from it.

The Derbyshire *volume in the famous series of Shell guides to the English counties was written by the renowned travel writer Henry Thorold and illustrated by distinguished photographers including Edwin Smith and John and Edward Piper.*

HENRY THOROLD *A Shell Guide: Derbyshire* (1972)

The . . . central area runs from the valley of the Derwent to the valley of the Dove, and comprehends the great stretch of moorland that lies between. It is the limestone area, the Low Peak, or if you prefer the name, the Wapentake of Wirksworth. Through limestone a river drives its channel deep, or even quite often underground. The Derwent valley is narrow, and at Matlock is little more than a gorge; but the Dove Valley from its source to Ashbourne is far narrower, and far too narrow, thank heaven, for a road. The Dove accordingly pursues its way in peace, while the Derby to Buxton road is forced to follow roughly in the tracks of the old Roman road, clean over the high ground. Extraordinary country it is, too – a country of ancient quarries and still more ancient mines, scattered over with the remains of old superstition in barrows and lows and circles of stones, and sprinkled with bleak inhospitable villages, where immemorial customs and beliefs are dying harder than anywhere else in Britain.

Finally there is the High Peak, the great barren area of gritstone that lies north of a line from Buxton to Chesterfield. This is the Derbyshire that one comes to see – the countryside itself – where London seems a thousand miles away. This is the land of loose stone walls, of vast areas of peat, of tors and edges and caverns and waterfalls. This is the paradise of the claustrophobe, where he can set an unlimited moor against an unlimited sky. This country is appreciated much, but it is a marvel that it is not appreciated more . . . Why, one feels, motoring over the Snake Road, less than two hundred miles from London, why go further afield?

Peveril Castle, with a snow-clad Mam Tor behind

Arthur Hopcraft, author, journalist and playwright (1932–2004) was the man who brought George Smiley to our screens with his adaptation of John Le Carré's Tinker, Tailor, Soldier, Spy *(1979), one of the most successful TV serials ever made. He was also well known for his TV plays such as* The Nearly Man *and for his small-screen adaptations of* Hard Times, Bleak House *and* Rebecca. *He was formerly a* Manchester Guardian *feature writer and, like many contemporaries such as Patrick Monkhouse and Brian Redhead, knew the Peak very well. This was his contribution to* Village England, *an Observer book edited by Peter Crookston and published by Hutchinson in 1980.*

ARTHUR HOPCRAFT *Village England* (1980)

Snobs have a phrase for it: day-trippers' paradise. And so it is. Praise the Lord and pass the Thermos.

The Peak District is like some gigantic version in natural, rural form of that most urban of English creations, the garden rockery. It is roughly 40 miles long, north to south, and at its widest the best part of 20. The top end, geographically, is also the higher, just clearing 2,000 feet. Some rockery! But its position supports the analogy. It is circled by the back doors of Manchester, Oldham, Sheffield, Barnsley, Derby and Stoke, to name but the largest of the industrial communities which dearly need the garden of the Peak. Given a sunny weekend or bank holiday they claim it by the drove, producing a confluence of dialects that puts the foraying visitor from distant parts – say, Birmingham – properly in his place as an outsider, however amiably received.

Close proximity to so many densely populated towns has had important effects on the Peak District. The crucial battles for the right of public access to open country (nationally) were fought here, sometimes physically: rambler versus gamekeeper, occasioning actual bodily harm. There was need for spectacular mass trespass, back in the days of hobnails, before legislation freed the splendidly wild tracts of Kinder Scout and Bleaklow to coming generations who now tread as they wish – or as the maze-like topography of these strange plateaux dictates.

These northern heights of the area are the most dramatic features of what is called the Dark Peak: not by reason of some mysterious truncating of the hours of daylight as against those enjoyed by the southern section, known as the White Peak, but because of the characterizing gritstone rock. Gritstone is a severely clerical grey in the kindest weather. In the grimmer sort it can look sooty black, so that you navigate from one weirdly rearing landmark to another, plunging in and out of deep peat-ditches, utterly black, like the wandering hero from some early moonshot serial of tuppenny-rush times.

There are rocks like huge black mushrooms, cotton reels, egg-timers, capstans, thumbs, boots, anvils, One set is called the Boxing Glove Stones, and the name is aptly descriptive. These oddities are peculiar to the place, just as the words for certain other natural aspects of the landscape are. A 'clough' is a valley. Those peat ditches are 'groughs'.

The guidebooks, quite sensibly, emphazise that the Kinder and Bleaklow plateaux can be dangerous spots in bad weather, even though their altitude and their shape seem hardly to justify reference to them as 'mountains'. The point is that they often demand the use of map and compass even from the devotees who walk them obsessively. Kinder has the bigger following, with the exquisite cul-de-sac village of Edale at its foot and the choice of numerous walks which can begin and end there without retracting of footsteps.

The village is a cosy huddle in a broad green vale, worth a visit merely to look at: something indefinable in the scale and arrangement of buildings against setting. True, there is now a sizable car park, plus public lavatories; but this was a necessary piece of tidying-up, rather than 'development', and it left the village itself unmolested.

Edale is the southern starting point of the Pennine Way, A little purpose-built bridge across the gurgling Grindsbrook stream replaces the felled tree that used to set walkers off on the 250 miles to the Scottish border. Crossing Grindsbrook at this point does not, of course, render an obligation to keep going for the two weeks that the Pennine Way commonly requires. Countless carloads of the elderly frail, the infantile and the perfectly hale and lazy simply wander on a couple of hundred yards to find a picnic spot and perhaps dip their toes in some chilling little ring of bright water. You can day-trip to Edale very pleasantly. You can ski there, too.

The title 'cradle of English rock-climbing' is generally attributed to the Lake District, and more particularly to Wasdale Head, from where debonair Victorian gentlemen – they had to be gentlemen, otherwise they would not have had the leisure to make the journey or the money to afford it – disovered exhilarating sport on Great Gable and Pillar. But it is a fair argument that the Peak District provided the nursery for modern English climbing. The reason, again, is the simple fact of the Peak's accessibility to places where a lot of people live. Two of the legendary figures in post-war mountaineering, Joe Brown and Don Whillans, took their first steps towards extraordinary activities in the Alps and Himalayas by grappling inquisitively with the odd 40 or 50 feet of upright Peak gritstone.

Brown went looking for light and air not available to him in one of the gloomier bits of Manchester. Whillans found it equally necessary to break out of Salford. They have reason to be specially grateful for the Peak; but in this they are merely the most famous in a multitude who hold a lifelong attachment to the district and the airy adventure it so readily offers.

Peak District rock-climbing gives plenty of scope to the novice, but it also provides some alarming challenges to the most expert. The extra merit of the latter category, as far as the non-climber is concerned, is that you may just chance to get a close-up view of one such brute being tackled as you pause in a stroll from your parked car. There is a considerable thrill in this, it may not need to be said – except that the excitement is heightened by a sense of privilege. The climber is not putting on a show: he is practising his special skills for the personal satisfaction of it.

On a brilliant May Sunday I turned about 20 yards off a popular footpath, hoping to find climbers in action on the crags overlooking a valley road with its straggle of houses and muffled traffic, nose-to-tail. Sure enough there were the expected little groups of serious faces, much red rope, crash helmets and some cautious work to give relaxed entertainment. Then quite casually a lone youth appeared at the foot of something no one else was attempting, and began moving upwards. He was dressed in denim shorts and a singlet, with no rope, no helmet. Clearly he was merely trying out a couple of moves, and would drop back to earth again in a moment or two. He did not. He went up and up. A little bag of chalk dangled from his belt at the small of his back, and between moves he dipped his fingers into it. That was his only aid to security as he progressed from one scratch on the rock to another, until ending the climb with a couple of little diagonal hops.

It was a piece of private athleticism of dazzling ease. I suggested to the other climbers that what I had just watched may have impressed them, as well. They agreed. They checked with the guidebook and said the climb was graded 'exceptionally severe', beyond which difficulty of ascent a man needs wings. This sort of climbing also happens elsewhere, of course, but it is particular to the Peak District that it can be happened upon quite so effortlessly.

Men with wings were, in fact, hovering in the sky not far away at the time – hang-gliding is the newest of Peak sports. On the same afternoon a village cricket match close to the hotel where I stayed at in Baslow featured the ghost of W.G. Grace, bearded and vast-bellied and showing signs of grumpiness in the heat. Had I wished, I could have gone underground to admire electrically floodlit caverns. Instead I took a walk along a lane running beside the River Derwent, where the noise from the main roads was abruptly gone: small enterprise hugely rewarded.

It is roughly around Baslow where the gritstone begins to give way to the limestone that provides the southern part of the district with the name of the White Peak. In strong sunlight the drystone walls have the gleam almost of snow. This is pastoral, wooded country, very gentle on the eye. In contains villages and hamlets which make a virtue of aimless meandering: usually a no-nonsense pub, probably a photogenic hump-backed bridge over a glinting stream with a 'private fishing' sign, and a tranquillity to play tricks with your sense of time. Arguably, the definitive White Peak meander is to drift southwards from Hartington to Dovedale, through Beresford Dale, Alstonefield and Milldale, and then north again via Tissington. The old railway lines hereabouts have been turned into grassy tracks – the ironware removed – so that one may now walk along winding, gentle gradients, springy under foot and often banked around head height on both sides.

A good base from which to 'do' the Peak? Bakewell is an exceptionally attractive small town, with a resplendent Gothic-arched bridge over the River Wye. And it has a notably good bookshop – thereby satisfying my personal test of small towns worth a linger.

Another former Guardian *writer, and a resident of Rainow on the western edge of the Peak, was Brian Redhead, the acerbic Radio 4* Today *presenter, founder of the jokey 'Friends of the M6', and later an inspiring and outspoken president of the Council (now the Campaign) for National Parks.*

BRIAN REDHEAD *The Peak: A Park for all Seasons* (1989)

I first set my eyes on the Peak District on a Saturday, and I was working. It was in July 1954, and I had joined the reporting staff of the *Manchester Guardian* the previous Monday. It was the day meat came off the ration and my first assignment was to go to the meat market, where I reported that the return to private enterprise created chaos and panic. There was no bidding. The wholesalers named their prices and the retailers simply shouted their assent.

On the Saturday I went to Buxton. I went by train and I could not believe what I was seeing through the carriage windows. I had crossed the Pennines by train before, on the Leeds, Huddersfield, Stalybridge and Manchester line, so I knew a Pennine town when I saw one. But this was different. Even from train level, which is not to be compared with riding the roads let alone with scaling the heights, I saw at once that this was like nowhere else.

I had seen more remote places – the Cheviots as a child; I had seen more beautiful places – the Lake District as an evacuee; I had seen more exotic places – the Far East as a National Serviceman; but I had never before been so taken by surprise by a landscape. One minute I was in the suburbs of Manchester and the next in this most open of open countryside.

And from that day to this, whenever I drive up into the Peak I never fail to get that same feeling of surprise at being so suddenly on top of the world. To live on the edge of the Peak, in Sheffield or in Derby, in Stockport or in Manchester, and, of course, in Macclesfield, is to have delight on your doorstep. It is the great escape.

On that first Saturday I was in Buxton to report a speech to an audience of teachers by J. Chuter Ede, a Labour politician of great wisdom and charm. Back in the office on the Sunday afternoon I wrote my report, which in the tradition of the *Manchester Guardian* was as much about me as about him, and then I held forth in the reporters' room about the wonders of the Peak.

The Deputy Editor, P.J. Monkhouse, was in charge that night and hearing my innocent enthusiasm invited me into his room, once the leaders were safely set, and told me that the Peak was a Park. He was too modest to mention that his book *On Foot in the Peak*, published more than twenty years earlier, was one of the great manifestos of the outdoor movement, and it was only later that I discovered that he was a founder member of the Peak Park Board.

But I swiftly learned that the *Manchester Guardian* was the house journal of the National Park movement, to such an extent that when leader writers were stuck for a final sentence on any subject they were always tempted to write: 'But the situation on the Peak Park Board is acute.'

Years later when I succeeded Paddy as Northern Editor of the *Guardian*, I too added my pen to the debate, but in those early days in Cross Street I was more concerned to explore the place as distinct from the arguments.

At the end of that July my wife of a few weeks arrived in Manchester from Newcastle, having completed her teaching term in order to qualify for her holiday pay. She had £38 10s, and with it we bought our first car.

It was a 1932 two-seater Rover convertible. At least that was what it had been but, when we bought it, it had neither seats nor hood. However we had it fitted with an old bus seat and a pram hood (there was no MOT in those days) and off we went to explore the Peak.

The roads were quieter then than they are now. The serious walkers still arrived by train, and even those out for a run in the car on a Sunday parked and walked; they did not just park and eat.

We, I confess, roared along the roads, making a noise which I would deplore now. The Rover had a six-cylinder engine and a deep-throated exhaust which made it sound both more powerful and faster than it was. It also had a strange transmission system with a worm drive, and any careless use of the clutch could break a half-shaft – which was why I always carried two spares.

But if we rushed up every valley from Longdendale to Dovedale, we also stopped and looked – at Chatsworth and Haddon Hall, at the caves and the caverns, at Mam Tor and Axe Edge, at Ashbourne and Bakewell, at Edale and Eyam.

There was it seemed no end to it. We came to understand, as everyone who knows the Peak comes to understand, that you can go there every weekend of your life and not exhaust it. It is not a place to visit now and then; it is a place to enjoy always.

Edwin Drummond is a poet and one of the more controversial rock climbers of the 1960s–1980s, famous for his performance art poetry readings and protest climbs on notable public buildings, such as Nelson's Column in 1978. But he was also a fine rock climber, responsible for many first ascents of classic routes, such as the eponymous 'A Dream of White Horses' on North Stack, Anglesey in 1968. This is his account of his first ascent of the 'Easter Island' route on the limestone fang of Ilam Rock in Dovedale in 1973, taken from his autobiographical A Dream of White Horses.

EDWIN DRUMMOND *A Dream of White Horses* (1987)

EASTER ISLAND

I'd always wanted to go there. I had a picture. Incredible, a tusk-white rock, tropical, like Treasure Island: childhood . . .

Hamish loosened his grip – immediately my loins felt the cool draught. He leaned back. I didn't say anything. Besides it was stopping and we'd soon be there. Leaving Sheffield, the gravelly rain had turned to big blots of snow going through Chatsworth, then to a fuzz, here and there a wet, white feather. By the time the Honda purred to a standstill, the air was warm, the sun was shining and the snow lay in tatters on the fields, its wave passed.

The world remade. Shakespeare's though, not Christ's even though it was Easter Sunday morning. Magpies flashing through the trees; blackbirds noisy as parrots; a gold finch simmering for rose hips; dippers weaving in and out of the small waterfalls the Dove made slipping over the stepped river bed. An English jungle. Not a soul about. I felt like Thor Heyerdahl. Ilam, it sounded Samoan.

Jesus Christ! Scary, lonely. It looked more like Thor's blood-spattered anvil, up-ended centuries ago in the forest. Something was dripping. A white patch of snow drooped over the summit like a flag.

Well. We can have a look. Hamish followed. He'd been pretty quiet. Three years now we'd known each other. Tall, pale, chivalrous; though he'd never been in any of my dreams, an anchor in the waves I tended to make. Now he had to decide what to do. University? Work for his father? From the street outside his house, I could see half a bedroom wall being taken up by the Mt. Everest he was painting. I would miss him.

Ilam Rock, Dovedale

The face leaned over us. I felt like a painter in a shipyard.

'Where's the ladder?' But neither of us laughed. I looked up: Proctor country . . . I'd climbed a bit with Tom. Gentle, mild-mannered as a shire. Once he'd told me of a wild birds' egg collection he'd made as a boy. Every bird you could think of, hundreds and hundreds, from the lapis of a robin, the ivory nut of a wren, down to a peewit's muddy nugget. He had the crown jewels of Derbyshire in his bedroom, all correctly named and labelled, with the discipline of a mathematician, the patience of a painter. And to watch him climb! Taxonomic down to the fingertip, it was as if he was standing on eggs: so deft, and unbelievable his strength, you felt he could crush holds, yet he floated up. When he put his glasses on he looked like Clark Kent. And, though I never told him so, by his side, I felt like Lois.

I was clinging to the edge about fifteen feet above Hame's head, trying to get my foot up, onto a tufty hold in a little dish.

It was like trying to shave while driving.

'Watch me –' He licked his lips. I'd found a scalloped edge, about as thick as the handle on a British Railway's tea mug. I had to go. I started pulling out – if it broke I'd be thrown back onto the station. Pitons clanging I started moving.

'We're off!' I yelled.

The Dove was steaming. The sun was directly above now, hammering down. The rock was as dry as a freshly ironed white collar, and, for a while, I just stood, at the bow of myself again, swaying gently.

'How are you doing?'

'Hamish, I think – '

I felt like an angler with three rods. To my left, a ripple of incuts led to a gash, a crack – but no footholds. Not having Tom's thumbs up for power moves, my feet would be like wheels. Nevertheless, I made a few perfunctory twitches with my left hand: 'Too steep.'

Too deep. Ahead of me, the arête rolled up like a wave. And I wasn't a strong swimmer. Though I've crawled like a snail where some, stronger climbers have got butterflies and drifted back down. So I went more to the right. A bit of knees-up Mother Brown to get me over the bulge – I pulled my horns in, slithering rapidly back.

A family was having a picnic across the river. I was being watched . . . I looked away. Defensive, pinched for holds, with my hands in the air above my head, like I was being held up. Eyes searched me. Climbing is strange. We want to get away – from different things – but once beyond the lawn, the cat, mail in the morning, her face across the table, we can't go too far, because they wouldn't be there. I turned around. And waved, because they were there, interested, happy, like ponies in the sun, having a rest. They'd probably earned it.

So. Back to work. The problem is – like darning: Appliqué yourself Drummond. The rock is a fabric. There are holes in it. But I need repairing – I put in a pin. There, that won't rip. And I start weaving – will's the loom – shuttling back and forth, fine lines of feeling, hemming an atoll from the waves, tucking the loose ends in, fingers bobbing up and down, a bit of sewing machine leg – Then, strange as ripples, after making a splash, coming back – the sinking feeling disappears and I strike out of fear and elation, one wave that carries me up onto Whillans' shoulders, Brown's head and, with a quick pull on the Crew's halo, I'm poised, on the crest, diving for a jug, dark eye of a needle deep in the rock. It accepts my hand like a letter box slot. Snarling a bit I rush out to whoops and barks from Hamish.

A group of climbers had arrived and were passing around a pair of binoculars. I was battering out old wooden wedges from the summit crack, hanging on a fist jam like a drunken sailor. The ropes billowed out below on the white sail of the rock. This was to be our last climb. Hamish would go on to study Philosophy, headstrong on Logical Positivism, getting higher at Aberystwyth. And, after three years teaching, I was leaving school too. By the time he graduated, and began shipping second-hand cranes to Norway, I'd had my Gaugin-like pretensions stripped away by a beautiful and abused native of the States, the same age as him, whom I was to meet in Yosemite. But that's another story.

The wind was just right. Not a cloud in the sky. I could see the green waving in the distance. We were almost there.

Jim Perrin is undoubtedly among our finest modern writers on the outdoors. What makes his journalism and other writing stand out from all the others is that he makes it obvious that he really cares about what's happening – and being allowed to happen – in our precious countryside.

Born in Manchester, Jim started climbing in the Peak District at the age of twelve and became one of the leading British rock climbers in the 1960s and 1970s. He is a regular contributor to many daily newspapers and outdoor magazines, and has won the prestigious Boardman-Tasker Prize for Mountain Literature on two occasions. The following two essays are from Jim's regular column in the magazine TGO.

JIM PERRIN 'Book of Changes', *TGO* (December 2001)

> 'Kinder Scout is a mountain. It has to be taken seriously.'
> – Patrick Monkhouse, *One Foot in the Peak* (1932)

How many miles is it, I wonder, from Leygatehead Moor to Crookstone Hill? Six? Seven at most, I suppose. And from Sandy Heys to the Madwoman's Stones it's significantly less than that, with the greater part of it at about the two-thousand-foot contour. But what stretches between is out of all proportion to distance and height. What stretches between is Kinder Scout, and it's one of the great, vital and unique wilderness areas in these islands.

I hear a whisper of derision from Scotland and Wales at that description. It's misplaced. These moorland rough heights of the Dark Peak you take lightly at your peril: the sucking peat, the slithering descents and panting scrabbles out again from mirey groughs, the disorientations of mist, the disobliging set of the land against whatever direction your objectives may lie in, the shelterless terrain, the long descents – you think these insignificant? I remember the scout boy in his thin clothes sprawled in the Alport River, just across the Snake Road to the north, dead, and his companions dead likewise on the moor above, that they were racing over on a March day when the snow swept down before a bitter, unfettered wind from the north, in my youth, and the days off school searching for them.

In my Manchester youth, this was my first mountain, and I took it most seriously. A quick, cheap train-ride out to Hayfield and, barely beyond the city's boundaries, you were at its foot. Hence its necessity, that didn't equate with availability until the great Socialist open-country legislative programme of the late 1940s and early 1950s, to which we, as hillgoers, remain vastly and perpetually in debt. ('*It should be remembered that all ways up Kinder Scout are trespass and that consideration of the feelings of the grouse, if of no-one else, suggests a certain discretion – to say no more – in the choice of seasons for the excursion.*' Patrick Monkhouse, 1932 – and consider how relevant this latter date is. It was the year when Benny Rothman and his companions sacrificed months of their liberty to ensure decades of our freedom to roam - here on Kinder Scout specifically, emblematically, but also on wild land throughout Britain. Look on the Dark Peak map now and there – above the name of Kinder Scout, in larger type still is emblazoned their banner and their bequest to us, for which they defied the law and took their bruises from the sticks of landowners' lackeys: *Access Land . . . !*)

I feel an extraordinary strength of attachment to this – mountain? I know what Monkhouse means when he calls it by that name, but in truth it doesn't sit easily. For although Kinder has many of the attributes of a mountain, it has a uniqueness of form and a singularity of character that somehow break down the term into a more complex entity. Grindsbrook or the Crowden Brook, Fairbrook (‘*a magnificent water course, almost worthy to drain the slopes of Beinn MacDhui – and the Cairngorm streams are the best I know*’ – Monkhouse) or the River Ashop could certainly be approaches – and very worthy ones – to many a grand mountain, but they don’t broach this one’s mystery. To the earliest travellers around its precipitous ramparts, ‘the great plateau within remained unseen, unguessed at, and unnamed. You cannot see it, until you are on it. There is no vantage point from which to look down and see the whole of it.’

I suspect that even among the majority of our present-day outdoor community, this situation still obtains. The paths that skirt the perimeter widen yearly into tracks, are maintained and defined and paved and even, in one or two appalling instances, signposted (I consider that we, as responsible hill-goers, have a moral obligation to destroy any sign or supernumary and recent cairn we come across on high, open land, in order to protect those who would feel empowered by their fallacious support from embarking on expeditions to which their capacities and experience are not adequate). But those that lead into the interior are fainter, less noticeable, more wandering. A blue hare – the mountain hare that turns white in winter, and was mercilessly harried once by the shooters up here whose activities excluded us for so long – lopes mildly away to lead you along them; an errant migrant of a snow bunting scurries, startlingly conspicuous, across the black hags of eroding peat; in front of you on a clear, cold autumn night, suddenly the glittering interplay of the Northern Lights illuminates the sky, searing above valleys gauzed by industrial haze.

Where do they take you, all these lovely, natural signs? Ah! They take you to nowhere. Look on the map again. Barely a couple of names or the wriggle of a single contour line to each of those grid squares across the plateau. ‘Kinder Scout – The Peak – its summit lies at 2,088 feet (636 metres) above sea level . . .' the guidebooks will tell you. Its summit . . . ? Do they know? Go to its supposed summit for yourself. Its bird-limed, lop-sided little cairn totters out of a peaty pool along the line of a low ridge five hundred metres north-west of the great winged rock that's Pym's Chair. Stand on the margin of the pool and by some trick of perspective the rocks all along the plateau rim seem to rear above you. There's barely a hundred-foot difference in elevation all across the long miles of Kinder Scout.

There is nothing here, and when you come from a place where everything crowds in, therein lies much of its appeal. This place, when I was a child, was a revelation to me. It bespoke spaciousness, emptiness, the impersonal, as it reared up as eastern bulwark to a blackened city wherein everything was threat. From the windows of my school library, there it was, stretched out 'like the ramparts of paradise'.

And of course, I was terrified of it. I've written before of setting out from Hayfield as a solitary just-turned-twelve-year-old in the spring of 1959, barely skilled in the use of map and compass, intending to reach Edale by way of Tunstead, Kinder Low and the wild, shelving, spacious edge past Noe Stool, The Woolpacks and The Anvil. I didn't make it. As I laboured along Kinderlow End and past the Kinderlow Cavern towards the Ordnance Survey pillar beyond where the ridge abuts the rim, tongues of mist flickered and rolled from off the plateau, raced down the hillside towards me as though animate. I fled before them, along the flank of the Swine's Back and down to the sheepfold at Edale Cross, where I sheltered and brewed up tea on my primus and sweetened it with Nestle's condensed milk from a tube – do they still make that extraordinary sweet concoction? – and wondered if the gamekeeper Patrick Monkhouse described ('. . . on populous Sundays a gamekeeper may be seen sitting with a dog and gun on the side of South Head. His presence is usually an adequate deterrent, and the gun has not yet been used') was still, little more than a quarter-century on from Monkhouse's time, lying in wait for unwary ramblers?

This for me was a defining moment of mountain experience. I would not be exaggerating if I were to tell you that I was terrified. And just as I had had to master fear as a child on the rough streets of Hulme, or in the gym where my father took me as a six-year-old to learn to box, or later when I sought it out on the great cliffs, so in this moment I had to come to terms. But not to the extent that on this day I went back into the mist. Instead, I clattered down the stony runnels of Jacob's Ladder and trailed along the sequence of footpaths into Edale in the eternal rain. And next day, when it cleared, tentatively, fearfully, momentously, I crossed the plateau from Grindsbrook to Kinder Gates and the Kinder Downfall for the first time, finding my way, losing my heart to the place.

This was over forty years ago, and in the book of changes that is Kinder Scout my eye discerns much that is altered in that passage of time: the regimentation of approaches to the hill, the paths paved with gritstone setts from the defunct cotton mills of the north, the Groundwork Trust's and Manpower Services Commission's and National Park Authority's and National Trust's initiatives that were Margaret Thatcher's ambiguous legacy to this landscape; the increased popularity; the erosion of the peat away from the rim; the gentrification of the hill-farming hamlet that was Edale . . .

Though much has changed, much remains the same. With my good friend Beatty I went up there on a glorious soft day of autumn a week or so ago, the air motionless and warm, thick and filmy down in the valleys but of singing clarity above the fifteen-hundred-foot contour. We drank tea on the step outside Cooper's Café in hot sunshine, took the field-paths that are the low-level alternative Pennine Way route out of Edale village, branched off into Crowden Clough, and up that we climbed, the gentlest and most gradual of ascents by the side of what Monkhouse terms 'sweetest of all the waters on Kinder'. It's an exquisite little stream, its heather banks ornamented here and there by rowan and ancient holly trees, its final gorge almost impressive before it debouches on to the wild plateau in an abstract patterning of water-gleamed and foam-laced strata.

When you've arrived here, the hard work is done. The sun glints and glitters on crystals in the rough grits of Crowden Tower, the valley falls far away beneath, the plateau-rim undulates along all the way round to the Downfall and beyond. And we linger along it too. Among the Woolpacks, wind-sculpted shapes of millstone grit (most abrasive of all rocks and most endearing to the northerner born) detain and enrapture with their hipped and lipped and bosomy roundnesses. A lone woman rambler walks towards us, greets us and passes into the thicket of them, the soft mobility of her flesh like rippled reflection as she moves on through. Beneath an unnamed buttress that would be chalked and polished and worn away by the climbers if its location were more amenable to their indolence, John and I sit on springy green turf that has long gone from the base of the more accessible gritstone edges, share flasks of coffee, watch the sun sinking into the bruised skies of Manchester and bloodying them as it does so. We visit the cosmically wonderful summit, its cairn crystal-rendered in the pool beneath. We laze back, Pym's Chair behind us against the sunset like some strange, awkward bird settling to roost, the red moor-grass all around flaming in the afterglow. We cut across to Grindslow Knoll and The Anvil, splash down the mirey shoulder above Broadlee Bank, and descend this as the dark falls, remembering – remembering how much this hill has meant to us, and to all like us, who made it their escape.

JIM PERRIN 'Use and Abuse', *TGO* (April 2006)

To feel and speak the astonishing beauty of things
– earth, stone and water,
Beast, man and woman, sun, moon and stars –
The blood-shot beauty of human nature,
its thoughts, frenzies and passions,
And unhuman nature its towering reality –
For man's half dream; man, you might say,
is nature dreaming, but rock
And water and sky are constant – to feel
Greatly, and understand greatly, and express
greatly, the natural
Beauty . . .

– Robinson Jeffers

In a spirit of nostalgia I walked up to Stanage Edge on a perfect February Sunday because this place for me was where so much that has been crucial in my life first took shape. As a young climber, I remember being awakened by daylight here on my first outdoor mornings as I slept on a bed of bracken I'd gathered from the slopes below and carried up to the *Grand Hotel*, as the chiselled name above the wonderful, wind-carved pocket of Robin Hood's Balcony Cave at Stanage calls it, and where generations of young Peakland climbers and walkers had slept before me. I remember slithering in my sleeping bag across the sandy floor, out of the entrance, over to the lip of the ledge. The cold air of morning on my bare shoulders caused me to shiver a little and shrink down into my warm cocoon. In front of me, from the pupa and chrysalis of the night the butterfly day was emerging. There was a sea-wash and a swirl of white mist in the valley floor, visionary. It was all in motion, vaporous tongues licking at elephant peaks which lazed on a white savannah: Win Hill, Lose Hill, Bleaklow were all stretched out there, bolstered into individuality with the sun not yet risen behind me so the colours were muted – but they came, and the bracken crackled aflame among spectrums of heather, mist boiled in the day's retort and distilled, suggestion resolved into form, all this alchemy happening before my eyes in the mornings of my youth, with my life before me and the whole day's journeying and play ahead. I remember it so well, and the feeling it engendered in me, the need.

On this February Sunday in the present year the noon air was crisp, the crag sunlit, and no-one was climbing on it. I exaggerate slightly here, because when I walked down through the plantation below *Fairy Steps* and *The Unconquerables* and scanned along the crag, I did make out a couple of parties on easy routes along the whole four-mile-length and crest of the country's prime and foremost 'rock-climbing recreational facility', as the authorities who now have governance and control over our relict tracts of wilder country might term it. The boulders scattered throughout the plantation were, of course, packed – hundreds there, a whole stadium-crowd of the mattress-carriers who constute climbing's largest current sect going through their curiously static and mimetic routines, daubing the rock with chalk all the while so that all the boulders have come to resemble nothing so much as an inner-city, monochrome graffiti-site (I was talking with my dear old friend of over forty years, Joe Brown, about the use of chalk in climbing yesterday. He is beyond any rational dispute the greatest climber Britain has ever produced, and his view of it is that chalk in climbing is unnecessary, an environmental atrocity, a form of cheating that marks and reveals the mysteries of a climb for those too timid to discover for themselves. But ambitious self-interest has ensured that argument long since lost . . .)

Ten years ago, on a day like this, it would have been the crag that was thronging. As at any time and in any weather over maybe the last fifty years of the recreational explosion. Seeking consolation, rather than inevitably depressive explanation, I tell myself it's great, that the grass is growing back under the crags (it is!) where I used to laze between climbs years ago, that the ring-ouzels will be returning, replacing the climbers (getting them banned from here by the RSPB, too, of course), that sweet old nature's getting her chance to breathe undisturbed. Except that that is not the case: all morning there was been the whine of transmissions and rumble of big diesel engines and screech of motor-bikes as the 4WD fraternity (sic!) and the scrambles-bikers graunched and jounced up and down the Long Causeway that runs from below High Neb on to the top of Stanage by Count's Buttress.

Let me step aside from this rhetorical thoroughfare for a few moments and make some crucial observations. Quite simply, I would rather not engage in the controversies that are generated around environmental issues. Inevitably, it seems to me, they degenerate on the one side into lofty cat-calling in the arcane dialect of an exclusivist, careerist tribe called *the conservationists* (many of whose so-called *management schemes* are as pernicious in their effect as the straightforward damage of irresponsible recreational abuse), and on the other into extremely nasty and bullying rallies and sallies expressive solely of preservation of interest. On the latter, I recall that twenty years ago I wrote a piece in this magazine about scrambles-riders in Wales desecrating some of that country's loveliest and most remote ancient trackways. The comeback on it was dire: vilification in their interest-group magazines, misrepresentation, packages of dogshit through the letter-box, anonymous phone-calls and letters issuing death-threats against my kids and myself (I took legal action against the misrepresentation and – true to form for these blustering cowards – the apology was immediate and craven. As to the anonymous stuff, those who can't square up to you openly are never worth worrying about).

High Tor, Matlock Bath

These machine-driven folk are cross, competitive people. When you attempt to limit to socially-harmonious modes their particular pursuits insofar as they jeopardize the pleasure of the whole nation, they come on pretty nasty and the person who voices the complaint ends up a bit like an Asian corner-shop owner at a *British National Party* rally – the pack slavering, waiting to see who first dare bite before they all pile in. Look at some of the correspondence in *TGO* that my fellow-columnist and friend Mike Harding has received over the years when he's written on these issues. For my own part, the stance to which I'd worked round over decades – and after many years in which I did actively and militantly campaign against the serious threats to our environment posed by the military, water-privatisation, the fixing in agricultural and silvicultural interest of our major environmental agencies, the irresponsibilities and deceits of bodies like our National Trusts – all battles long lost the effect of which is written in dire terms on our present landscape – was that the best individual effort and contribution I might make as a writer to the preservation of landscape beauty was by celebrating it, wherever I came across it and in the integrity of my individual consciousness.

Well, I'd like again to take you back a few decades. I remember the Long Causeway as it was when I first came to Stanage, which is fast closing on fifty years ago now. I remember even twenty years ago it was a slow-ascending, historic trackway, guttered and drained, kerbed and cobbled with gritstone setts. It was beautiful in a way that David Jones defines in his seminal essay on 'The Utile' from *Epoch & Artist* – craftsmanlike, integrated, perfectly attuned to the purpose for which it was intended (which did not comprehend motor-vehicle-usage). If this piece of masterful civil engineering had been a building, it would rightly and properly have been listed and protected.

It should have been, for now it's a rubble-filled, eroded gully. Soon its buttressing will collapse. In one instance from this bright Sunday, I saw eight 4WD vehicles descending it in close formation, nose to tail, and a couple more on the way up. A dozen or so had passed me when I'd walked up part of the track an hour or so earlier. I'd peered in through wound-up windows at their human complements of jowly, beer-bellied, shaven-headed, combat-fatigues-clad drivers and obese children, and been a little amazed, as well as poisoned by their exhaust fumes. Then I'd turned down the old pack-horse trail into the plantation, which was a serious hazard zone for an idle old pedestrian like me, because a hyper-gaggle of mountain-bikers were doing serious damage to their penile nerves and storing up prostate trouble for their advancing years by whizzing down it and then grinding up it again repeatedly – all illegally, because this is not a bridleway – in thigh-straining, wobble-wheeled slow-motion. But they weren't doing as much damage as the 4WD lot, so long as you kept out of their way . . .

Their way . . . ?

I know that in our limited countryside we have to share our recreational amenities, and if there were any suggestion that exclusions should be considered, I'd be as quick as anyone to look at them sceptically, to view them askance. Nor do I much like models such as the American or Canadian, where regimentation and the enforcement of access-quotas is the rule. But it seems to me that the notion of sharing within any society is dependent on the Rousseau-istic idea of a contract into which we enter voluntarily for mutual security and good, and which should comprehend respectful use of all joint amenity. The drivers of off-road vehicles – who clearly have a current *legal* right to practice their activity in the rare and precious environments of our national parks, thanks to the anomalous survival of historic highway designations – have equally clearly and demonstrably been guilty of an extraordinary and prolonged act of vandalism which has destroyed a beautiful and historic feature. They will get away with this scot-free, morality and legality being in this case, as so often, poles apart. If I were to take it into my head to smash the fountains at Chatsworth and cut down the rose-gardens at Haddon Hall, I'd end up in gaol. That is the equivalent of what the drivers of *Shoguns* and *Fourtraks* and *Discoveries* and *Hi-Luxes* have done to the Long Causeway, and unlike what I've just imagined at Chatsworth and Haddon, their damage won't be made good.

All this experience leaves me wondering whether our outdoor-representative bodies are making any noises at the moment about the need for a social contract – initially consultative and voluntary, but with the long-term goal of legal revision and codification – for the environment? Problem for me in all this is that like most climbers and outdoor-goers of my generation I'm an old-style libertarian anarchist who finds it hard to respect authority in any degree. I love the crags, the hills and moors, the wild places and creatures, and want to see them preserved, but the people who take on the role of policing them seem almost inevitably to grow pompous and rigid and authoritarian. It's like the body-language of those whistle-suckers in black who rush up and down football-fields flashing red and yellow cards – don't much like them, they interfere with the game, are open to abuse and error and prejudice, but please can we have a few for each of the National Park Authorities to hand out on-sight red cards to all the 4WD-fantasists who – imaginations fuelled by colour-supplement advertisements – seem to think that they're ploughing through some impassable and remote wilderness right on the outskirts of Sheffield city-limits on their way to get themselves and their blubbery brood a fat and beery lunch within the ersatz cosy of the *Fox and Harrow* in Shatton-under-the-Moor before buggering up another remnant of relatively unmarred, relatively wild space on their way back home to Dore or Dronfield where they'll spend the remnants of the Sabbath day stuffing themselves with more processed gluttonies, watching *Coronation Street*, and then the pub and porn after their desperate, uncherished wives and machine-fed children have gone to bed:

> The beauty of modern
> Man is not in the persons but in the
> Disastrous rhythm, the heavy and mobile masses, the dance of the
> Dream-led masses down the dark mountain.
>
> – Robinson Jeffers

They will roll anyway down their materialistic, exhibitionist, pseudo-mountain-trail; but I wish, in doing so, they would not so wear away, so defile, our rare and common spiritual and historical and natural resource. As for me, I'm glad I've spent my life 'Married to the massive/Mysticism of stone./Which failure cannot cast down/Nor success make proud' rather than to the internal-combustion engine. That's from Robinson Jeffers again. I don't think he liked people very much, preferred a falcon on the whole: 'Fierce consciousness joined with final/Disinterestedness.'

I begin to see his point . . .

BIBLIOGRAPHY

William Adam, *The Gem of the Peak*, Longman & Co, 1843

E.A. Baker, *Moors, Crags and Caves of the High Peak*, John Heywood, 1903

Thomas Bateman, *Vestiges of the Antiquities of Derbyshire*, John Russell Smith, 1848

______, *Ten Years' Diggings in Celtic and Saxon Grave Hills*, George Allen and Sons, 1861

Ann Beedham, *Days of Sunshine and Rain: Rambling in the 1920s*, published by the author, 2011

'Strephon' [Edward Bradbury], *In the Derbyshire Highlands: Highways, Byeways and My Ways in the Peake Countrie*, J.C. Bates,1881

Edward Bradbury, *All About Derbyshire*, Simpkin, Marshall & Co, 1884

Charlotte Brontë, *Jane Eyre*, 1847, reprinted by Oxford University Press, 1998

Eric Byne and Geoffrey Sutton, *High Peak*, Secker & Warburg, 1966

William Camden, *Britannia*, 1586

Arthur Conan Doyle, *The Terror of Blue John Gap*, 1910

Eliza Cook, *Derbyshire Dales* (1860?)

Charles Cotton, *The Wonders of the Peake*, 1682

James Croston, *On Foot Through the Peak*, John Heywood, 1868

Daniel Defoe, *Tour Thro' the Whole Island of Great Britain*, 1726, reprinted by Dent, 1962

John Derry, *Across the Derbyshire Moors*, Sheffield Independent Press, 1934

Michael Drayton, *Poly-Olbion*, 1622

Edwin Drummond, *A Dream of White Horses*, Diadem Books, 1987

George Eliot, *Adam Bede*, John Blackwood, 1859

Ebenezer Elliott, *The Poetical Works of Ebenezer Elliott*, Henry S King, 1876

Celia Fiennes, *Through England on a Side Saddle*, 1698, reprinted by Penguin Classics, 2009

Ethel Bassett Gallimore, *The Pride of the Peak*, Jonathan Cape, 1926

Luke Garside, *Kinder Scout and the Footpaths and Bridle Roads about Hayfield* Seeley, Jackson & Halliday,1880

Sally Goldsmith, 'Trespassers Will be Celebrated', unpublished, 1992

John Hillaby, *Journey through Britain*, Constable, 1968

Thomas Hobbes, *De Mirabilibus Pecci*, 1636

Arthur Hopcraft, *Village England*, Hutchinson, 1980

Louis J. Jennings, *Rambles Among the Hills*, John Murray, 1880

C.E.M. Joad, *The Untutored Townsman's Invasion of the Countryside*, Faber & Faber, 1946

Ewan MacColl, 'The Manchester Rambler', 1932, from *The Essential Ewan MacColl Songbook*, Oak Publications, 2001

S.P.B. Mais, *The Highlands of Britain*, Richards Press, 1932

______, *This Unknown Island*, Falcon Press, 1933

Hannah Mitchell, *The Hard Way Up*, Faber & Faber, 1968

Patrick Monkhouse, *On Foot in the Peak*, Alexander Maclehose, 1932

Carl Philip Moritz, *Journeys of a German in England*, 1783, reprinted by Jonathan Cape, 1965

Jim Perrin, 'Book of Changes', *TGO* magazine (December 2001) and 'Use and Abuse' (April 2006)

Crichton Porteous, *Derbyshire*, Robert Hale, 1950

______, *Peakland*, Robert Hale,1954

Roger Redfern, *Rambles in Peakland*, Robert Hale, 1965

______, 'Alderley Edge', *Guardian* Country Diary, November 8, 2011

Brian Redhead, *The Peak: A Park for all Seasons*, Constable, 1989

Ebenezer Rhodes, *Peak Scenery*, Longman, Hurst, Rees, Orme, Brown and Green, 1824

John Ruskin *Fors Clavigera*, George Allen, 1896

Henry Thorold, *Derbyshire*, Faber & Faber/Shell, 1972

Thomas L. Tudor, *The High Peak to Sherwood*, Robert Scott, 1926

Alison Uttley, *The Farm on the Hill*, Faber & Faber, 1941

George H. Wilson, *Some Caves and Crags of Peakland*, Buxton, 1926

Francis A. Winder, *An Unconventional Guide to the Caverns of Castleton*, W. Hartley Seed, 1938

William Wordsworth, 'A Tradition of Oker Hill', 1829, in *The Complete Poetical Works of William Wordsworth*, Macmillan, 1888

______, 'Chatsworth', 1835, in *The Complete Poetical Works of William Wordsworth*, Macmillan, 1888

INDEX

ACKNOWLEDGEMENTS

The author and publisher are extremely grateful for permissions to publish extracts from the many books used in the compilation of this anthology. Particular thanks to due to Jim Perrin, the estate of the late Roger Redfern and Guardian Newspapers, the estate of Brian Redhead, Ewan MacColl Ltd, Edwin Drummond, Ken Wilson formerly of Diadem Books, Ann Beedham, and all the other authors and publishers of the books from which extracts have been included. Every attempt has been made to trace copyright holders, but we hereby acknowledge any which may have inadvertently been omitted.

Particularly thanks are due to my good friend Karen Frenkel, for the marvellous modern photographs which grace this book. And as ever, I owe most of all to my wife Val, for her unswerving support and love over our nearly fifty years together. This book is dedicated to her.